Hans Bgd

God's Awesome Challenge

God's Awesome Challenge

Harold C. Bennett
Compiler/Contributor

Broadman Press
Nashville, Tennessee

Robert B. Williamson
A dedicated Christian layman
Encourager
Challenger
One . . . as my father

Contents

Preface

The purpose of this book is to inspire God's people to become involved in God's world mission enterprise.

Each chapter treats one of the great themes inherent in the challenging facets of Bold Mission Thrust, the most far-reaching and ambitious mission and evangelism program ever adopted by the Southern Baptist Convention and, perhaps, by any denomination in the history of Christendom. Southern Baptists have committed themselves to tell every person in the world about the love of God in Jesus Christ by the year 2000.

To share the gospel with the 4.2 billion people in the world within the next two decades is only possible as God empowers his people to accomplish that which he has placed in their hearts. Faith, as a grain of mustard seed, and total life commitment are required.

In 1978, during the annual meeting of the Southern Baptist Convention, the Convention voted enthusiastically to adopt Bold Mission Thrust 1979-1982. Acting upon a recommendation from the Executive Committee of the Southern Baptist Convention, Albert McClellan made the motion, and the Convention adopted the following program purpose, objectives, and goals.

SOUTHERN BAPTIST CONVENTION
BOLD MISSION THRUST

Purpose: That Southern Baptists understand, accept, and become involved in the mission to enable every person in the world to have opportunity to hear and to respond to the gospel of Christ by the year 2000.

In order for this purpose to be fully realized, the churches must make spiritual preparation. This preparation must include praying, strengthening the church membership in Christian growth and discipleship, and applying the gospel in the community and in society at large.

Objectives and Goals (1979-1982)

I. Bold Growing . . . by providing New Testament based churches and missions for all people . . .

(1) Through increasing Bible study enrollment in existing churches by 12 percent by 1982.

(2) Through providing opportunities for all persons in their localities to hear the gospel resulting in an increase in baptisms of at least 10 percent per year through 1982.

(3) Through establishing 5,800 church-type missions and churches.

(4) Through every church establishing at least one point of witness in new geographical and/or cultural areas.

II. Bold Going . . . by seeking out and equipping the called and cooperating in the support of persons participating in the activities of Bold Mission Thrust . . .

(1) Through churches seeking out the called and supporting 1,000 additional career missionaries.

(2) Through the churches seeking out the called and cooperating in the support of 5,000 Mission Service Corps and 100,000 other short-term mission volunteers.

(3) Through churches enlisting and equipping church members for presenting the gospel in their own localities.

III. Bold Giving . . . by providing adequate financial resources to accomplish Bold Mission Thrust . . .

(1) Through enlarging the financial base in each church by at least 15 percent annually.

(2) Through doubling gifts through the Cooperative Program by 1982 (from 1977).

(3) Through enlarging gifts for work through the associations by at least 10 percent each year.

(4) Through increasing the special mission offerings; foreign, home, and state, by at least 10 percent each year.

(5) Through securing adequate gifts over and above regular gifts to send 5,000 Mission Service Corps volunteers.[1]

In Houston, Texas, at the annual meeting of the Southern Baptist Convention, June 12-14, 1979, the Convention acted upon a motion of Harold C. Bennett and adopted a recommendation from the Executive Committee of the Southern Baptist Convention continuing Bold Mission Thrust for 1982-1985 with emphasis content as follows.

Bold Mission Thrust
Matthew 28:18-20

"Southern Baptist efforts are focused on involvement in the mission to enable every person in the world to have the opportunity to hear and respond to the gospel of Christ by the year 2000. Such involvement in a Bold Mission Thrust requires responsible action through the church in order to reach people, develop believers and strengthen families.

Reaching People

"An organized, intensive and coordinated global (worldwide) effort of missions and evangelism to enlist new people into the kingdom of God and church membership, and to establish new fellowships of believers.

Developing Believers

"Responsible Christian growth resulting in witnessing to lost people, ministering to people in need, especially the economically, socially, and physically deprived, and committing life and financial resources to God's kingdom through the churches.

Strengthening Families

"Affirm the biblical concept of the family and respond creatively to problems of deteriorating marriage and changing patterns of family life."[2]

May God grant us his grace and power as we share the gospel with every person in the world.

> Harold C. Bennett, executive secretary-treasurer
> Executive Committee, Southern Baptist Convention
> Nashville, Tennessee

[1]Recommendation No. 17, *The 1978 Annual,* Southern Baptist Convention, Atlanta Georgia, June 13-15 (Nashville: Executive Committee, Southern Baptist Convention, 1978), pp. 47-48.

[2]*Bold Mission Thrust Bulletin,* August 1, 1979, p. 1.

Harold C. Bennett has served as the executive secretary-treasurer of the Executive Committee of the Southern Baptist Convention since August 1, 1979. He is a native of Asheville, North Carolina and a graduate of Southern Baptist Theological Seminary.

1
GOD'S AWESOME CHALLENGE

Matthew 28:18-20

Not many months ago, my wife and I were on a mission tour to South America, Africa, and a part of Europe. It was an exciting, thrilling, and challenging experience.

Something happened in Asuncion, Paraguay, which caused me to ask myself, again, *How can we reach the world for Jesus Christ?*

Unfortunately, our flight schedule into Asuncion missed the connection with our next flight, and it became necessary for us to spend the night in Asuncion, Paraguay. This disappointed us. We were unhappy with the airlines and the world! In checking through customs, we discovered that no one there could speak English. From a variety of people, we tried to find out when we could catch the next flight to Rio de Janeiro. Nobody understood our language. After we finally found a young lady who could speak English, we were delighted to talk with her. She explained that the next flight to Rio would be on the following day and that the airline would house us overnight in a downtown hotel and then see that we got back to the airport in time for the flight. It sounded very accommodating.

To our dismay, we learned that no one in the hotel could speak English. We had a meal ticket, but no money with which to buy a cold drink. We could not drink the water for we were already ill from that practice. I stood looking out the window at the river, only two blocks away. The view was interesting, but not beautiful. I glanced down at the main street of the city and watched the hundreds of people milling in and out of the shops. I thought, *How can we reach these people when I cannot even speak their language?*

My mind wandered back over the years to the time when we were in Tokyo, Japan, to attend the Baptist World Congress. On Sunday morning, a group of us wanted to attend church service which would require a ride on a train. A. V. Washburn, former secretary of the Sunday School Department of The Sunday School Board of the Southern Baptist Convention, knew where the train station was located but none of us was prepared for the mass of humanity getting off the train. There were eight or ten of us who were halfway up a wide staircase when a train stopped on the upper level. It seemed like thousands of Japanese got off the train and descended the stairs. We stood to the side and let them have the right-of-way. I could see over their heads. It looked like a great river flowing down the stairs. There were hundreds, perhaps thousands, of people.

I thought, again, *How can we share the gospel of Christ with all of the people of the world?*

Nevertheless, the Great Commission is clear. Jesus said, "All power is given unto me in heaven and in earth. Go ye therefore, and teach all nations, baptizing them in the name of the Father, and of the Son, and of the Holy Ghost: Teaching them to observe all things whatsoever I have commanded you: and, lo, I am with you alway, even unto the end of the world" (Matt. 28:18-20).

Some of us have heard this commission and read these words so often that we have become blasé about them. The words sometime fall on the deaf ears of people who have lost the vision of the lost world. The whole experience is lacklustre and no longer excites us.

The Bible is definite in that it is God's plan for God's people to be a blessing to the nations of the world. The universal purpose of God was made clear when he spoke to Abraham, promising to make of him a great nation and promising that "in thee shall all families of the earth be blessed" (Gen. 12:3). This thought refutes Macbeth, who assumed that long life was "a tale told by an idiot, full of sound and fury, signifying nothing."[1]

His Power

Before Jesus outlined God's awesome challenge, he made one of the most astonishing claims of his entire ministry. A. T. Robertson pointed out that Jesus "spoke as one already in heaven with a worldwide outlook and with the resources of heaven at his command. His authority or power in his earthly life had been great. Now it is boundless and includes earth and heaven."[2] I do not feel that Jesus would have given the Great Commission to his followers unless he had received power sufficient to enable those receiving the commission to accomplish his bidding.

All of us have experienced the power of God. First of all, we experienced his presence and power when we first believed in Christ as personal Lord and Savior. It is through God's power and grace, by way of our personal faith, that we are able to experience forgiveness of sin and to receive everlasting life. The power of God is manifested in the resurrection of Jesus Christ from the tomb. In Ephesians 1:18-19, Paul expressed in his prayer the hope that the Christians at Ephesus would *know* the hope of God's calling, the riches of his glory, and the exceeding greatness of his power.

However, there is always a danger of judging the power of God by our own personal experiences alone. Permit me to draw a parallel. During the years I lived in Florida, I learned something about the ebb and flow of the tide of the Atlantic Ocean. The tide was always evident, always there, and always powerful. I was impressed by the tide because I owned a small boat. The incoming tide would lift the boat and gently lower it again as the tide flowed out.

The tide was powerful enough to lift my small boat, but there is a greater fact to be considered. That same tide is powerful enough also to lift all of the navies of the world. Any battleship or aircraft carrier or small rowboat can be lifted by the tide. We face the danger of misjudging the power of God. Although we know his power, it is not limited to our knowledge.

Jesus said that his power was boundless and therefore he was going to send his people on a mission to the world. A. T. Robertson wrote:

It is the sublimest of all spectacles to see the Risen Christ without money, or army, or state, charging this band of 500 men and women with world conquest and bringing them to believe it possible, and to undertake it with serious passion and power. Pentecost is still to come, but dynamic faith rules on this mountain in Galilee.

Our Lord expects us to respond to his commission by doing what we can. We must do our part in the world mission cause of Christ. John R. Bisagno, pastor of the First Baptist Church of Houston, reminds us of some of the inspiring words of Winston Churchill during World War II. In a sermon entitled "The Power of a Positive Influence," Dr. Bisagno tells of a group of coal miners who went to Winston Churchill with the request that they be permitted to volunteer to go to the front and fight. They were discouraged and felt that their lot in life was unimportant. The next day, a meeting was arranged in Royal Hall and Winston Churchill arose to address the four thousand miners in attendance.

"Gentlemen, they say he [Hitler] is coming. They say he has 100,000 men on the sea, 100,000 on the land, and 100,000 in the air. But, I say to you that one day we are going to be victorious over this matter and one day we will walk down the streets of London in victory and I will say to a young soldier, 'Where were you in Britain's finest hour?' And he will answer, 'I was in the trench with my rifle fulfilling my responsibility, doing my part for my country.' And, I will say to a wife and mother, 'Where were you in Britain's finest hour?' She will say, 'I was in a hospital caring for the wounded, fulfilling my responsibility and doing my part for my country.' And, I will ask some of you where you were during Britain's finest hour and you will say, 'I was down in the pit of the mine with my face against the face of the coal, fulfilling my responsibility, doing my part for my country.' "[4]

His Commission

Jesus is positive in his commission, "Go ye therefore, and teach all nations" (Matt. 28:19). The assignment is clear, we are to go into all the world and preach the gospel to everyone, everywhere.

Not only is it the duty but also it is the privilege of every follower of Jesus Christ and of every church to make disciples of all nations. It is not possible for the missionary effort to succeed apart from the involvement of individual Christians who have had a personal experience with Jesus Christ. "It is the duty of every child of God to seek constantly to win the lost to Christ by personal effort and by all other methods in harmony with the gospel of Christ."[5]

The population of the world is awesome. I cannot even imagine the size of a group of people numbering only one million. Nevertheless the latest estimates of world population is 4.2 billion persons. The shocking truth is less than 25 percent of the world's population can be classified as Christian, even by the most liberal definition of Christian.

Yet, Jesus Christ died for everyone in the world. Read again these verses of Scripture: "For God so loved the world, that he gave his only begotten Son, that whosoever believeth in him should not perish, but have everlasting life" (John 3:16); "To wit, that God was in Christ, reconciling the world unto himself, not imputing their trespasses unto them; and hath committed unto us the word of reconciliation" (2 Cor. 5:19); "But God commendeth his love toward us, in that, while we were yet sinners, Christ died for us" (Rom. 5:8); "And he said unto them, Go ye into all the world, and preach the gospel to every creature" (Mark 16:15).

It is true that the use of the word *world* in the Scriptures has a variety of meanings. The meaning depends upon the context. In biblical terminology, the *world* might refer to the universe as a whole, to the earth, to the world system, to the whole human race, to humanity minus the believers, to the Gentiles in contrast to the Jews, or to believers only.[6] However, in defining the meaning of the word *world* as it is used in the Great Commission, A. T. Robertson stated that the *world* is "the whole cosmos of men, including Gentiles, the whole human race."[7]

Is it not incredible that our Lord would ask us to go into all the world and preach the gospel! That depends on how great a God we believe in. Henry Norris Russell of Princeton University was one of the most distinguished astronomers of his day. On an occasion, he was asked by a woman how he could be a scientist and also believe in God. In response to the letter of inquiry about the matter, Dr. Russell wrote: "It would represent me more accurately to say, 'Madam, that depends on how great a God one believes in, and on whether one can trust Him regardless of changing theories about details.' "[8]

With a commission like our Lord's commission, there is little reason for wasting time. Christians cannot afford the luxury of a casual attitude about the work of God through the churches.

This significant truth is pinpointed by a humorous experience. A number of years ago, I was traveling across Florida to a preaching engagement. It was about midmorning and I had been driving for several hours. While passing through a small town in the central part of the state, I stopped at a restaurant for a coffee break. Sitting on the far side of the restaurant, next to a window, I noted that there was only one other couple in the restaurant at the time. They were talking quietly, and I was thinking about the message I would be delivering within the next few hours.

I glanced across the room at the couple, and they had summoned the waitress to the table. The elderly couple pointed to a glass of water in the middle of the table. It was a plastic glass and evidently it was leaking. She peered at the glass and then took her glasses from her pocket, put them on and looked at the glass closer and closer. She straightened up, removed her glasses, returned them to her pocket and with a smile on her face, said to the man, "This is a small town and there is not much to do, so people come here and just sit around and watch the glasses leak!" What a great response! But, God's people dare not take the time to sit around and watch leaking plastic glasses! We have too much to do.

His World

In giving the commission to those gathered on the hillside that day, Jesus not only included the Jews but the Gentiles as well. As a matter of fact, the commission did not limit the geographical location for the missionary activity of his people. It included the entirety of the world.

On April 11, 1970, I had the opportunity of being present in Florida for the launching of Apollo 13. It was a thrilling and unique experience. I shall never forget the excitement of the day. Prior to, and following, that experience, Americans have had the satisfaction of knowing that we were the first on the moon. A new truth came to me from a preacher friend of mine who was as excited as I in watching, via television, the first astronauts walk on the surface of the moon. He said, "Did you see what happened up there? Did you really see what was going on?"

I said, "Yes, I saw it, but what are you talking about?"

He said, "Although walking on the moon, the astronauts were in fact walking in the atmosphere of Earth. In a similar manner," he said, "God's people walk on the Earth but they walk in the atmosphere of heaven."

I had never thought of it just like that. But it is a significant truth. This is God's world and God's universe. God's Son, Jesus Christ, who is our Lord and Savior, has asked us to preach the gospel everywhere in the world. This is his awesome challenge.

In order to accomplish this assignment, we must have a strong home base. I believe in a strong home base, but I do not mean that we should have a home base to the exclusion of the world mission program.

About 150 years ago, Alexis de Tocqueville (1805-1859), a French politician and writer, made the statement, "America is great because she is good, and if America ceases to be good,

America will cease to be great.'' I feel the same way about our great denomination. I believe we have become great because we have had a heart to share the gospel with the people of the world. If we ever cease to be missionary in spirit and practice, I believe we will cease to be great.

In thinking about the millions of people in the world, we may overlook the fact that each one must become a Christian on an individual basis, one at a time. We must find a variety of ways to share the message. Each person must make a personal decision to accept Christ for himself.

As a case in point, a number of years ago, Darold H. Morgan, president of the Annuity Board of the Southern Baptist Convention, had an experience in New York City which illustrates the need to share the gospel with individual persons. The following testimony by Dr. Morgan, entitled "Christ on Wall Street," appeared in the June 4, 1973 issue of *The Illinois Baptist.*

"Someone left this Gospel of John on your back seat," I said, calling the driver's attention to the little paperback, which had a pamphlet tucked inside it.

"I put it there," he answered.

"I want you to know how much I appreciate finding it," I told him. "I'm a Christian and it means something to me."

"I'm a Christian too," the driver commented. "I've driven a taxi in New York City for 20 years. This is how I witness."

The driver proceeded to tell me how the Gospel of John, which bore the emblem of the American Bible Society, and the tract, telling how to find Christ as Savior, always evoked conversation. "Some of my women fares," he said, "you can tell are having some problems. They ask me to pray for them."

Not every rider reacts favorably. Once a colorful trial lawyer, grabbing national headlines for defending a group of demonstrators, boarded his cab.

When the famous attorney saw the Gospel and tract, he demanded with disgust, "What's this? Who put this here?"

"The Spirit gave me the boldness to reply, 'I put it there,' " the driver recalled.

"Well, I'll have nothing to do with it," the passenger shot back. "I've always managed for myself and I always will."

"There'll come a time, no matter how famous a lawyer you are, when you won't be able to take care of yourself," I told him. "When you stand before the judgment bar of God without Jesus as your Savior."

"Oh, don't give me any of that," the attorney retorted. When this distinguished passenger got out, he counted his fare carefully to the exact penny. "He didn't even give me a dime tip. But I gave him something. I gave him the Word."

"It's not my job to make Christians of them. It's only my job to witness to them, to sow the seed," he observed.

The driver said, over the years, he'd given out 25,000 copies of the Gospel of John and more than 40,000 tracts on how to be saved.

I started to get out as soon as we reached my destination. The driver stopped me. "Do you have time for us to pray together?" He clasped my hand and on Wall Street involved me in a powerful moment of intercession.

After I'd left the taxi, I thought of the verse commanding us to be "witnesses in Jerusalem." Here was this taxi driver, in what I consider one of the most difficult locations to have an impact for Christ, witnessing effectively in a way that only a taxi driver could.

His Teachings

Jesus said to go into all the nations, "teaching them to observe all things whatsoever I have commanded you" (Matt. 28:20). The teachings of Jesus Christ are important, and it is mandatory that as God's people we spend sufficient time in teaching the Word of God. This is not a ho-hum assignment but a privileged responsibility that requires our best.

The apostle Paul said, "And I, brethren, when I came to you, came not with excellency of speech or of wisdom, declaring unto you the testimony of God. For I determined not to know any thing among you, save, Jesus Christ, and him crucified" (1 Cor. 2:1-2).

In his sermon entitled "Our Bicentennial," Billy Graham, related an experience of Alexander Solzhenitsyn. Mr. Solzhenitsyn told of an experience which magnifies the importance of the cross. He said that only once during his long imprisonment in a Soviet Union labor camp did he become so discouraged that he contemplated suicide. He was outdoors on a work detail. He had reached the point where he didn't care whether the guards killed him. When he had a rest break, he sat down and a perfect stranger sat down beside him. Someone he had never seen before and never saw again. This stranger took a stick and drew a cross on the ground for no explainable reason. Solzhenitsyn sat and stared at that cross, then said, "I realized therein lies man's freedom." At that point a new courage and a new will to live and work returned to him. The cross of Christ is central in New Testament Christianity and has the power to transform lives. It is the power of God unto salvation.

As we reach the people of the world, we must share with them the teachings of our Lord Jesus Christ. Jesus said, "Thus it is written, and thus it behoved Christ to suffer, and to rise from the dead the third day: And that repentance and remission of sins should be preached in his name among all nations, beginning at Jerusalem. And ye are witnesses of these things" (Luke 24:46-48).

His Presence

In accepting God's awesome challenge—the Great Commission of our Lord—we have committed ourselves to go to every person in the world. As we go, we have the remarkable assurance that Christ will be with us, for he said, "Lo, I am with you alway, even unto the end of the world" (Matt. 28:20).

"After this I beheld, and, lo, a great multitude, which no man could number, of all nations, and kindreds, and people, and tongues, stood before the throne, and before the Lamb, clothed with white robes, and palms in their hands" (Rev. 7:9).

Glory to God! He is with us! We do not walk alone! Amen.

Notes

[1] *Macbeth*, Act V, Sc. 5.

[2] *Word Pictures in the New Testament*, Vol. I, p. 244.

[3]*Ibid.,* pp. 244-245.

[4]E. Stanley Williamson, Compiler, *Faithful to the Lord,* p. 11.

[5]"The Baptist Faith and Message," p. 15.

[6]*Nave's Study Bible,* Revised and Expanded edition, (Nashville: Broadman Press, 1978), p. 1928.

[7]*Word Pictures in the New Testament,* Vol. V, p. 51.

[8]Andrew W. Blackwood, *Expository Preaching for Today* (Nashville: Abingdon Press, 1975), p. 166.

Landrum P. Leavell, II, has been the president of New Orleans Baptist Theological Seminary since January, 1975. He is a native of Ripley, Tennessee, and a graduate of New Orleans Baptist Theological Seminary.

2
THE PLAN AND PURPOSE OF GOD

2 Peter 3:9

Every generation has a golden moment in which to obey Christ's command to "disciple all nations." In the sweep of history, it appears that this is Southern Baptists' moment in life's little day, surely the last opportunity many of us will have to literally obey the Lord Jesus. God has given us the tool to use in reaching our world for Christ. Bold Mission Thrust traces its origin to the heart of God, for it is his will for none to perish, "but that all should come to repentance" (2 Pet. 3:9).

Surveyors of the contemporary scene have reminded us that Southern Baptists have halted their characteristic growth spiral. Though there are notable exceptions in individual states, the denomination as a whole baptized fewer people in 1978 than in many years. Some seek to explain this decline in terms of sociological changes. While there may be validity in this, the more precise answer will attribute the decline to disobedience!

It is true that churches face fierce and unrelenting competition from the media, mass sports, mass recreation, and an unprecedented affluence which provides most Americans with numerous options on Sunday.

We cannot return to the post-World War II or pre-Vietnam eras. Those halcyon days for the kingdom will not return. We may never see it again where lost people flock to the churches and readily respond to a gospel invitation. However, it is being proven in church after church across the length and breadth of the land that lost people are still responding readily to the witness of concerned Christians, and they are hungry for salvation. In the midst of the fierce foes that face us and the competition with which we must cope, the Spirit of God continues to pour out his power and give victory.

The Essence of God

God is love! In that brief sentence is found the profoundest thought ever to claim man's attention. One prominent theologian was asked the greatest thought his mind ever entertained. The response was, "Jesus loves me, this I know, for the Bible tells me so."

There is no such thing as unbestowed love. Love has an object. In the eternal purpose of God, man is his highest creation and the object of his highest love and devotion. Man has been entrusted with great authority and responsibility. God has assigned to man the task of dominion over the rest of creation. This is a tremendous revelation of the depth of the love of the Creator God, making us stewards over his creation.

Just as God's love for us is expressed, so our love for him finds an expression. The Bible reminds us that we love because he first loved us. The supreme expression of our love for him is found in explicit obedience to his commands.

God's love is so impelling that he instituted missionary outreach and became the first missionary himself. He sought Adam and Eve when they had sinned in an effort to bring them back to himself. That missionary outreach continued through the history of Israel, by means of prophets, priests, and kings. The fullest revelation of the essence of God came in the glorious consummation in Bethlehem's barn.

The first command of Jesus Christ to some fishermen was: "Follow me, and I will make you fishers of men" (Matt. 4:19). This revealed the pattern of his earthly life and for the lives of all his followers. The final command of Jesus prior to his ascension was: "As ye go therefore, disciple all nations." Between the first command and the last, Jesus constantly revealed the essence of God and his divine purpose.

Obedience to Jesus Christ in our day confronts us with a world population in excess of four billion. Even the most optimistic estimates would not indicate much more than one billion who are counted as Christians. It is understood that this one billion who hold membership in Christian churches have not all experienced the new birth. By a New Testament definition of salvation, many of these, maybe even a majority of them, do not know Jesus Christ in a personal experience of redemption.

That leaves three billion or more who acknowledge someone or something else as the lord of their lives. These constitute our prospect file.

It is a worthy exercise in discipline to remind ourselves that God loves those who are unsaved just as deeply as he loves us. This includes those of different cultures, different languages, and those who live on the other side of the earth. They are Muslims, Hindus, Communists, and even those who claim to have no faith beyond themselves. God loves each of them as well as those of us who are Anglo-Saxon protestants.

I recently read an article written by an associational missionary in which he defended the decline of churches in transitional neighborhoods. He warned that we must not apply the same standards of measurement to such churches as we apply to all others. I rebel against such a philosophy. Transitional churches have as great a responsibility to win the lost around them as any other church in any other neighborhood. The minute God accepts a man as his child, that man becomes my brother. If not, God is forsaken as Father. We can never win the world for our Savior if we are not willing to try to win those under the shadow of our church steeple. Transitional churches must become multiracial or deny the clear teaching of the Bible that God loves all men!

In Luke 19:10 Jesus stated his overarching task: "For the Son of man is come to seek and to save that which was lost."

Jesus Christ is perfect, totally without sin or error. If his purpose was to seek and save the lost, this then stands as the perfect and divine plan for the life of every follower. Our purpose as Christians is to be Christlike, hence the need for myriads of us to repent of our failure and our lack of zeal for the kingdom.

Power for the task of world conquest is ours for the asking. Jesus Christ has all authority, and he promised to be with us forever. All of the resources of the nature of God are available to us in carrying out the divine plan. When our Lord said, "All authority in heaven and on earth has been given unto me" (Matt. 28:18, RSV), he either meant all authority or he lied. He either possesses this power or he does not; and if he does not, we are of all men most deceived.

If this power actually resides in Jesus Christ, it is greater than any other force in the universe. His power is greater than a nuclear explosion, greater than all of the powers of Satan and the evil world, and greater than any power of evil men to deter and destroy. This power, which is the essence of God, is made available to his people for the accomplishment of his purposes. Only in that power can Bold Mission Thrust become a force and not a farce.

The Evil of Man

Man's evil is not always a lack of personal goodness. Actually, personal goodness may be the greatest enemy facing the Christian movement today. Lost persons by the millions are depending upon their morality and personal lives to save them. Often they are genial, generous, and gregarious. They regularly go to the polls, pay their taxes, and live in obvious affluence. However, the diagnosis of God is that they are depraved.

The depravity of man does not mean that there is no good in him. It rather means that he is incapable of doing what he was created to do.

Some years ago in Texas an inventor built a new and totally different kind of cotton picker. It was made of the finest and best materials that could be bought. Even the tires were the most expensive that were available. When it was completed, it was a thing of beauty and elicited innumerable positive comments. The only problem was that it could not pick cotton!

This is a picture of man's depravity. Having been created in the image of God with the sole purpose of glorifying him, man is incapable of fulfilling that purpose apart from divine intervention. This intervention is called salvation, or the new birth. Without it, man remains essentially evil in the view of God.

One group of social scientists who measure social change in America tell us that the new goals of the American people center in self-fulfillment. This is a focus upon self and a general spirit of entitlement. We are being warned that our society is fast becoming narcissist. This is a self-love culture, a society that looks continually in the mirror in admiration of itself.

We are told that this generation has a new "ism," termed "me-ism."

R. C. Halverson quoted the Frenchman, Emile Cailliet:

Self-centeredness is the essence of sin. Thus the self-sufficiency of man is itself the full measure of his solitude. Such a man is no longer addressable or answerable. He becomes, as it were, infected by evil. There at the core of his being, he comes into contact with a deep layer of hidden, unborn forces; with the collective unconsciousness from which he emerges in a proud god-almightiness. Like Faust's Mephistopheles, he henceforth embodies the spirit which denies everything held precious in the world.

A self-centered person becomes a little independent country bounded on every side by self. This is precisely the picture which

Isaiah drew of people going astray, each one turning to his own way.

All over the world there is pessimism concerning the future of mankind. We are extremely doubtful as to whether there is enough wisdom and moral rectitude among us to operate this complex society. The need for what Jesus Christ alone can give is at its zenith in human history. Humans without Jesus Christ are powerless to wage war with Satan and the forces of hell.

The Efficacy of Obedience

The plan of God, which is synonymous with God's will, is not illusive and hard to find. In fact, Peter said that God is "not willing that any should perish, but that all should come to repentance" (2 Pet. 3:9). Paul, in writing to Timothy, reminded us of the purpose of God in these words: "Who will have all men to be saved, and to come unto the knowledge of the truth" (1 Tim. 2:4).

Nothing could be more biblically authenticated than a relentless house-to-house, city-by-city, state-by-state, nation-by-nation effort to win people to faith in Jesus Christ. If we carry out the purpose of the Bold Mission Thrust, we will be carrying out the will of God. It is at the same time the most we can do and the least. It is the most because it encompasses the entire world. It is the least we can do because Jesus Christ commanded it.

Obedience to Jesus Christ involves praying that the Lord of the harvest will send forth laborers into the harvest. The need for volunteers is not limited to youth or those who have received prescribed formal training. The opportunities are without limit, and many retired persons are presently making themselves available. Young people are volunteering for the short-term mission opportunities. Others are ready to go, at their own expense, and serve in ways for which they are best suited.

There are churches across our denomination that have never sent out a young person committed to a church-related vocation. Pastors must give regular opportunities for people to make such commitments during the times of invitation. Sermons must be preached stating the opportunities that are available. Outside speakers must be enlisted to share the needs at home and around the world. Counseling must be done to help persons clarify and focus the direction in which God may be leading.

If we give Bold Mission Thrust our best effort, we have approximately twenty years in which to do the job. This will require the cooperation of every Southern Baptist. Perhaps the conflict will begin in an obscure fashion on a college campus. There are illustrations of other student awakenings that have motivated, challenged, and inspired. Wherever it begins, the match that starts the fire will be obedience. The ultimate test of the Christian faith is obedience. Jesus said, "If you love me, keep my commandments" (John 14:15).

Not long ago, the Dallas Cowboys and the Pittsburgh Steelers played the championship game of the year in Super Bowl XIII. Because of personal prejudice, I am convinced the Cowboys were clearly the superior team, yet they lost. The final score was 35-31. The Cowboys simply ran out of time.

During the exciting, closing moments of the game, Jackie Smith had the great opportunity and muffed it. The ball was thrown to him in the end zone. It hit in his hands. That touchdown might have won the game, or at least changed the outcome of it in some way, but he dropped the ball. He missed his golden moment. This life is the only chance we will ever have. We must not drop the ball.

Some years ago the University of Texas Longhorns were contenders for the national football championship. They had been rated number one by the press associations. In a particular game, they played the first half like untrained, junior-high-school football players. The opposing team had thoroughly outplayed the Longhorns. At halftime, a number of observers were wondering what the coach, Darrell Royal, would say to the team.

The halftime interlude was rapidly ebbing away, yet the coach had not spoken to the team. There was almost total silence in the dressing room, with only a few of the players moving around quietly. At what seemed to be the last possible moment, Coach Royal spoke quietly and said, "You're number one. Now go out and play like it." They did, and they won.

In the plan and purpose of God, people are number one. Let's live like we know that truth. The only way God's love is revealed today is through those of us who love him and obey him.

Perhaps we need to believe and apply the words of the well-known hymn: "O Zion, haste, thy mission, high fulfilling,/To tell to all the world that God is Light;/That He who made all nations is not willing/One soul should perish, lost in shades of night." All of us sing this heartily, and agree that this is right. However, it becomes more pressing when we sing the next stanza: "Behold how many thousands still are lying,/Bound in the darksome prison house of sin,/With none to tell them of the Saviour's dying,/Or of the life He died for them to win."

We finally reach the point of dedication and commitment when we can sing and mean the last verse. "Give of thy sons to bear the message glorious;/Give of thy wealth to speed them on their way;/Pour out thy soul for them in prayer victorious;/And all thou spendest Jesus will repay." That last phrase tells it all. There is no sacrifice we might ever make in obedience but that will be paid back many times over. One glimpse of our Lord in glory will cause all our trials and tribulations on this earth to pale into insignificance.

Herschel H. Hobbs is the pastor emeritus of First Baptist Church, Oklahoma City, Oklahoma, having served as pastor from 1949-1972. He was the president of the Southern Baptist Convention 1961-1963. A native of Talladega Springs, Alabama, he is a graduate of Southern Baptist Theological Seminary.

3
GOD'S TIMELESS MESSAGE

1 Peter 1:24-25

Daily newspapers reflect the transient glory of man. One day spectacular events are front-page headlines. The next day a small follow-up story appears on the inside of the paper. Usually, after that, nothing.

I am told that in the Louvre in Paris, France, there are at least three and a half miles of volumes on science which were once the latest word in that field. Now they gather dust and serve only to record the history of scientific groping for truth. A science teacher once said to me, "Any textbook on science that is *published* is obsolete. So rapidly does the field of science change, that we teach from mimeographed material prepared daily."

God's Abiding Word

The apostle Peter noted this changing scene when, quoting Isaiah, he said, "For all flesh is as grass, and all the glory of man as the flower of grass. The grass withereth, and the flower thereof falleth away" (1:24; cf. Isa. 40:6b-8a). The late Dr. Robert G. Lee was fond of saying that the glory that was once Greece is now but a piece of molded bread in the garbage can of history. Throughout Southern Europe and the Middle East decayed ruins of once mighty nations and civilizations serve to emphasize the Word of the Lord through Isaiah and Peter.

However, in sharp contrast to this, Peter added, "But the word of the Lord endureth for ever. And this is the word which by the gospel is preached unto you" or "the word, the one being evangelized unto you" (1:25; cf. Isa. 40:8b).

Word renders a verb (rhēma) which means "that which is spoken." In this case, that which God has spoken. Peter's combination of Isaiah's words with his added comment in verse 25b encompasses thè entire Bible, both the Old and New Testaments. So that in the Bible we have God's spoken word which keeps on abiding forever or unto the end of the age. Until the Lord comes again it will continue to abide as God's timeless message, heralding his will, warning those who defy it, and offering salvation to all who receive his Son as Savior.

The world is in constant turmoil and unrest. Moral values are regarded as relative in contrast to the absolutes of the Ten Commandments. Multitudes of people in an enlightened age spend far more time reading horoscopes than the Bible—if they read it at all. It is no wonder that the world wanders in a maze, seeking peace of mind and spirit—but never finding it. Why? Because they ignore God's sure and abiding Word to follow the ever-changing pronouncements of a groping materialistic science and the devil-inspired occult. We will never find the peace we seek until we find it in God who has revealed himself in both his written Word and his living Word—even his Son Jesus Christ.

What, then, may we say about the Bible?

God's Inspired Word

The Book or the Bible is made up of sixty-six little books *(biblia)*. They were written over a period of about fifteen hundred years in places all the way from Babylon to Rome. Their authors included kings, poets, prophets, priests, fishermen, farmers, a tax-collector, a physician, apostles, and other devoted servants of God. Many were unaware of the writings of others. None of them knew he was writing what would become a part of the Bible. Yet, when under the guidance of the Holy Spirit they were gathered together into the canon of Scripture, they tell a complete story. Andrew Melville said, "It is the wonderful property of the Bible, though the authorship is spread over a long list of centuries, that it never withdraws any truth once advanced, and never adds new without giving fresh force to the old."

None of these things can be said of any other body of writings. The only reasonable explanation is that these books had a common author, God, through the power of his Holy Spirit.

Samuel Taylor Coleridge once said, "I know the Bible is inspired because it finds me at a greater depth of my being than any other book." William Ellery Channing says, "The incongruity of the Bible with the age of its birth; its freedom from earthly mixtures; its original unborrowed, solitary greatness; the suddenness with which it broke forth amidst the general gloom; these, to me, are strong indications of Divine descent: I cannot reconcile them with human origin."

The Old Testament claims God for its author through human personalities (cf. Ex. 24:4; Jer. 30:2). Peter summarizes this in 2 Peter 1:21. "For the prophecy came not in old time by the will of man: but holy men of God spake as they were moved [borne along] by the Holy Ghost [Spirit]."

Even were there no evidence of divine inspiration elsewhere in the Bible, 2 Timothy 3:16 is sufficient to establish the fact (How often must the Bible say something for it to be true? Just once!). "All scripture is given by inspiration of God." Literally, "Every single part of scripture is God-breathed" *(theopneustos). Inspire* means "to breathe in." So God by his Spirit breathed into his chosen vessels the message to be delivered/written. Among Bible students there may be differences as to the method of inspiration God used. But among Southern Baptists there is agreement as to the product. It is God's inspired, inerrant Word.

The Baptist Faith and Message, adopted in 1963 by the Southern Baptist Convention, says of the Scriptures, "The Holy Bible has . . . God for its author . . . and truth, without any mixture of error, for its matter." With God as its author, and since it is "God-breathed," it naturally follows that it has "truth, without any mixture of error, for its matter." For God does not breathe error!

Some have sought to distinguish in the Bible between what is and is not Scripture. Thus they hold that only that which is Scripture is without error. Since I was the chairman of the committee which prepared the 1963 statement, as a revision of the 1925 statement, I have received much correspondence dealing with this fine point of interpretation. My reply has been that the question of separating Scripture from what some call non-scripture never arose within the committee. The statement on inerrancy definitely includes the entire Bible. The Convention which adopted it did so with this understanding. Since its adoption, subsequent Conventions have reaffirmed the statement, the latest at this point being in 1979. It did so following a statement by the writer that inerrancy applies to the entire Bible.

Of course, inerrancy refers to the original manuscripts. The Holy Spirit no more protects copyists from error than he does typesetters. Even so, the passages in question do not affect the message of the Bible. Past experience justifies us in seeing existing problems as due more to lack of full information and understanding than anything else.

The Bible is historically accurate. One of the most thrilling of stories concerns the role of archaeology in vindicating the historical accuracy of the Scriptures. In the multitude of discoveries throwing light upon disputed passages, not one time has one gone against the Bible. They have all authenticated it.

Furthermore, the Bible is scientifically correct. Of course, it does not claim to be a textbook in science. But no scientific error has ever been proved against the Bible. Some scientists and theologians may disagree. But true science and the Bible, never.

There is a vast difference between theory and fact. Scientific theories are a dime a dozen. In this category is found the theory of evolution. It has ever been and still is pure theory, even though some of its proponents present it as though it were a proven fact. If you repeat something long and often enough, no matter how false it may be, you will get many to believe it. You may even come to believe it yourself. But to propound theory as fact violates the basic principle of true scientific research which deals only with concrete evidence.

The Bible never discourages the exploration of new thought. It does not fear truth whether found in a text or a test tube. For both truths are of God. But beware of wandering into the trap of modern alchemy which by the waving of a magic wand of presupposition, without factual basis, would try to change theory into truth. This is no more successful than the ancient effort to change lead into gold.

By its very nature science must deal with cause and effect. In search for eternal verities, it must move backward from effect to cause. Eventually it comes to an effect (the natural universe and man) for which it finds no tangible cause. It is at that point that man must take the leap of faith as he says, "In the beginning God" (Gen. 1:1). And it is here that science ends and religion begins. This is where the Bible begins as it unveils God's revelation to man.

Shortly before his death, Dr. Arthur Compton, one of the world's foremost physicists, said that "in the beginning God" are the sublimest words ever penned. It is with this recognition that science must stand, and wonder, and should believe.

The late Harry Rimmer was a Presbyterian minister. He was also a recognized scientist, as evidenced by his membership in leading scientific societies in America and Europe. The latter part of his ministry was spent in writing and lecturing on the harmony between science and the Scriptures. He placed one thousand dollars in a bank and advertised far and wide that anyone who could prove a scientific error in the Bible could have the money. Through the years he received many letters pointing out such an error. But a letter setting forth both the scientific and biblical explanation satisfied the writers.

However, one man challenged him with a court suit. The case was tried before a judge and jury, with evidence presented according to the Rules of Evidence. The jury found in favor of the Bible.

Dr. Rimmer died with the thousand dollars still intact. If there are so many scientific errors in the Bible, as some suppose, why didn't someone receive that thousand dollars?

God's Timeless Word

Unlike the Moslems and their Koran, Christians do not believe that the Bible was written, bound in heaven, and handed down to men as a finished product. The Bible was wrought out in the arena of human history. It is God's history within history, as he reveals his eternal redemptive purpose amid the changing scenes of men and nations. It was forged in the hot fires of human need and struggle. Its written message was hammered out on the anvil of mankind's basic needs—economic, political, social, and spiritual. It was tempered in the roar of the rushing waters of a thundering, "Thus saith the Lord." And its message, even of God's wrath against sin, beats with eternal love for a lost and wandering race of men.

Since the Bible reflects the infinite wisdom of God, its meaning can never be exhausted by the finite minds of men. I was in Dr. A. T. Robertson's senior Greek class on Monday when a stroke was coming on him which took his life less than two hours later. On Friday prior to this he paid what was probably his greatest tribute to the New Testament. "I have been studying, preaching, and writing on the New Testament for over fifty years. But I never open my Greek New Testament but that I find something I never saw before."

In the seminary I learned many things from Dr. W. Hersey

Davis. But one thing has challenged me more than any other. He referred to the practice of preachers to deal only with the surface of the Bible, which has been scratched over so long that its meaning is obvious to most listeners. Said he, "Set your plow to go deeper, and turn up fresh soil which lies beneath the surface." Through the years I have found that there is an abundance of fresh soil, which makes the Scriptures live as never before.

Now since the Bible was wrought out in the arena of life, it spoke to the needs of those who first heard or read its message. But that message was not confined to them alone. The principles set forth apply to every person in every period of time. Outward customs and modes of life may change from generation to generation. But the inner needs of people remain the same. A modern man riding in an airplane at more than one thousand miles an hour needs God's message as much as did Abraham walking or riding a camel at three or four miles per hour.

God's Book is not dated. It was/is both timely and timeless in its message. To every age it tells whence we came, where we are, and where we are going. The present age of confusion needs to know all three.

For instance, the Ten Commandments are as binding today as when Jehovah first inscribed them on tablets of stone. Despite situation ethics and the so-called new morality, which is but old pagan immorality in modern dress, no person, society, or nation can defy the Ten Commandments with impunity.

Again, while predicting the future, the prophets also spoke to the sins and needs of their day. *Prophecy* means "to tell forth God's timely and timeless message as well as to foretell the future." There is no greater need today than for preaching from the Old Testament prophets as a mighty stream surging forth from the pulpits of the world.

People need to hear Amos as he thundered against political corruption, social injustice, and false religions. And as he called to "let judgment [justice] run down as waters, and righteousness as a mighty stream" (5:24). Also Hosea as in a succession of sobs he portrayed God's undying love for a faithless people. We need to weep with Jeremiah over our nation and world which seeks to avoid a nuclear holocaust. And we need to soar with the poet-prophet Isaiah as he pointed from despair to hope in God's Suffering Servant.

We need to feel the challenge of the Gospels as we view the Word become flesh to provide redemption for a lost humanity. We should know the fellowship of his sufferings, the power of his resurrection, his abiding presence in his Spirit, and to look up as we are filled with the blessed hope of his return in power and glory.

Every New Testament book has God's timeless message for us! Acts with its call to evangelism and missions; the epistles of Paul and others as they exalt and interpret Christ, dealing with problems which ever beset us, and fight the various "isms" which abide with us in modern sophisticated form. We need to learn from Hebrews the tragedy of lost opportunity if we ignore our place in the propagation of God's eternal redemptive purpose. And to exult in the promise of ultimate victory for Christ and his people, which is so vividly portrayed in Revelation.

No message is more needed for the Lord's people today than that of Revelation 4—5. John wrote in the context of persecution. Was Christianity to be destroyed? Would Domitian and Satan triumph over the Lord? Had God been dethroned?

It was in such a condition that the Lord said in effect, "Don't look about you as to what is happening on earth! Look up! And see what is happening in heaven!" Doing so, John saw that God was still on his throne. And Christ as the slain Lamb was still the Redeemer of all who believe in him. One interpreter says that in chapter 4 Jesus is saying, "Believe in God." In chapter 5 he is saying, "Believe in me."

Yes, the Bible is God's timeless message to every age—to our age. The masses of people need to hear this message. Men despair of the present and find no hope for the future. But God still says, "This is the way, walk ye in it" (Isa. 30:21). And that way leads to him who is "the way, the truth, and the life" (John 14:6).

Years ago Daniel Webster spoke words which were prophetic in nature. "If truth be not diffused, error will be; if God and his Word are not known and received, the devil and his works will gain the ascendancy; if the evangelical volume does not reach every hamlet, the pages of a corrupt and licentious literature will; if the power of the gospel is not felt through the length and breadth of the land, anarchy and misrule, degradation and misery, corruption and darkness, will reign without mitigation or end."

Ages past speak to present needs. These needs will be met only by God's timeless message. And he has charged his people with the responsibility of declaring it. If we fail, God has no other plan!

William M. Hinson has been pastor of the First Baptist Church, New Orleans, Louisiana, since May, 1977. He is a native of Miami, Florida, and a graduate of Southwestern Baptist Theological Seminary and New Orleans Baptist Theological Seminary.

4
CAPTURED BY GOD'S SPIRIT

Acts 1—4

My exciting city, New Orleans, loves monuments. One of the newer monuments was recently erected at the foot of Poydras Street on the historic Mississippi River. It is a statue of Sir Winston Churchill. When it was unveiled in front of the Hilton Hotel, one of our city leaders said, "Winston Churchill captured the imagination of war weary Great Britain. Because of his spirit and attitude, he was able to change the spirit and attitude of an entire nation that led them ultimately to victory in World War II, instead of succumbing to defeat."

As we read the first four chapters of the book of Acts, we see that the disciples of Christ sensed defeat after Calvary. They were more pessimistic than the people of Britain during World War II. But, their spirit and their attitude were changed dramatically by the time we get to the fourth chapter and see them boldly sharing their faith. Their whole life-style was dramatically changed. They were ordinary people (like you and me). Their lives seemingly had little order. There were no heroic attitudes exhibited within their ranks . . . but then . . . these people were changed! The thing that was lacking in their lives was provided and they began to realize extra-power for extraordinary living. Peter, who earlier shrugged his shoulders and said he was going back to his fishing, now stood up and preached with extraordinary power; thousands were converted (Acts 2:41). We read, "Daily they regularly frequented the temple with a united purpose" (Acts 2:46, MLB). They were now goal oriented and began to live by a new dynamic.

What happened? Methodist Bishop Gerald Kennedy wrote the introduction for a collection of the great sermons of Halford E. Luccock. As he extolled the great spiritual life and works of Luccock he said, "It is the gift of Christ to all who have been captured by His Spirit." I was impressed by three great truths in this introduction after I had read the entire book: (1) Great spiritual life is always the gift of Christ; (2) it is available to "all;" (3) who have been captured by his Spirit!

That is the answer! That is what happened in the lives of these disciples. They were literally "captured by God's Spirit." When they met together for fellowship and worship, "everyone felt a deep sense of awe" (Acts 2:43, Phillips). Great things were happening in this church. When faith dies, achievement dies! At the same time, when faith is boldly acted upon, God gives definite blessings that can be measured. This is revealed in Acts 2:41-47. The believers, Bible teaching and Bible study grew dramatically. The word "doctrine" in Acts 2:42 (KJV) is not passive, it is active. The proper phraseology would be, "They persisted in Bible study!" Their "fellowship" distinguished their gatherings. Great things were happening in this sharing church after they were captured by God's Spirit. Our First Baptist family decided to prayerfully let God's Spirit give us that great New Testament gift of *koinonia* (fellowship). We later adopted as our logo, for all printed materials, "The Fellowship of Enthusiasm." It was the result of the warm, growing fellowship of a Person within a person that is still overflowing beyond our walls when our service is telecast live. We pray for an ever-present spirit of expectancy when we gather for fellowship and worship that will thrust us out into our city as a living testimony for Jesus Christ.

The strategy in the Southern Baptist Convention has always been to make contact with the outsiders in our communities through our Sunday School. Since 1900 there has not been any other significant thrust that attracts, holds, nurtures, and leads individuals ultimately to a saving knowledge of Christ. This reached a marvelous expression of growth in the first ten years after World War II. It was during that period of time that we sort of bubbled over. We have glowing statistics to offer from that period of our history. Since then the evangelistic arm of the church has ceased to be as effective. But there is a new confidence and excitement throughout our country as God is at work. Bold Mission Thrust is being translated from a scriptural and spiritual challenge into the life-styles of individuals across this great land of ours.

We need to prayerfully move through the first four chapters of Acts and see what happens to a people when they are captured by God's Spirit.

The Holy Spirit Centered Their Basic Commitment

Every life has a center of gravity. Some refer to it as a "master sentiment of life" itself. As you read the testimony of the early church in Acts, you begin to grasp this truth in the commitment of these disciples. Jesus Christ became the focal point of their commitment. He centered their energies around himself.

Sometime after Calvary and before Pentecost, the disciples made a basic commitment to God. Before this experience they were without purpose. They were emotionally involved, but they were not deeply committed. This is basic. When we are captured by God's Spirit, we will commit all to him. There is a lot of talk about commitment these days. I have heard coaches urge their athletes to commit themselves to the task of becoming a winning team. I have read of the commitment of our American forefathers during the frontier days. Our church history is punctuated with the word *commitment*. The lack of commitment is realized in all institutions that travel the road of failure.

In the New Testament the word *commitment* is actually a banking term. It literally means "to give in charge as a deposit." We read in 1 Peter 4:19, "Commit the keeping of their souls to him in well-doing, as unto a faithful Creator." There were no banks when these followers of Christ heard that admonition. In fact, there were few safe places to deposit money or other valuables. These disciples regarded the word as "depositing money with a trusted friend." Such a trust was regarded as one of the most sacred things in life. Being captured by God's Spirit, they gladly committed (entrusted) all that they were and all that they had to God.

Our world is frantically seeking a "guaranteed deposit" in all areas of existence. Paul shared his commitment with his son in the ministry when he said, "Timothy, I am absolutely confident that God is a sound spiritual banker and that he has guaranteed my deposit of faith until the day of his return" (2 Tim. 1:12, author's translation).

That is it! Commitment is giving it all to him. I spoke before the prestigious American Bankers Association at their annual convention and shared Paul's testimony. I urged them to deposit (language that they understood) their faith in God through Christ. That is the only "guaranteed deposit" available to us in our world of transition.

Too many of our church people are for programs in words only. Many seemingly say, "Well, our last program didn't go so well, why don't we try this new emphasis and if it doesn't go . . . they will come out with another one and we will try it." Unless we commit ourselves to the controlling Spirit of God, we will die of physical exhaustion just trying out new programs.

We are educated out of our ears but not committed up to our ankles! Our problem is not that we lack the know how to reach the

world. We simply have not made that basic commitment to the call
of God in Christ to go.

I recently had the privilege of giving the welcoming address to
several hundred new American citizens in our Federal Court in
New Orleans. Before the naturalization ceremonies started, I
spoke to the clerk of the court of New Orleans. After determining
when I would speak on the program, I asked him, "How long have
you been leading aliens in their oath of citizenship?" He smiled
and responded, "I have rarely missed one of these naturalization
services in thirty-five years. I have three assistants that I could
send to take my place, but I would not want to miss the thrill of
seeing the hope written across the faces of the thousands of people
that seek to be free as American citizens. I mark my calendar and
commit myself to this task." As I reflected on that, I felt that the
Lord spoke to me and asked, How much are you committed to
witnessing to those that are alienated from me because of sin? Do
you receive a thrill when you see written across the face of a lost
sinner the joy of regeneration? I came away from that experience
knowing that I needed to give my life over to his charge, and that
called for a basic commitment.

The Holy Spirit Certified Their Brave Courage

With Christ at the very center of their new commitment, the
believers realized that his Holy Spirit endorsed with authority their
efforts to witness to the whole world. Jesus was not merely a
captivating new idea or philosophy. They had been captured by a
Person. The living God gave credence to their faith and witness.
They lived by a rare courage of commitment in the full power of
God's Spirit.

Their courage was marked by bravery. It is not redundant to
speak of their brave courage. William Barclay tells us that there
are two kinds of courage. "There is the reckless courage which
goes on scarce aware of the dangers it is facing. There is the far
higher, cool, calculated courage which knows the peril in which it
stands and which will not be daunted. It was that second courage
that Peter demonstrated to men "[1] After being captured by God's
Spirit, these people had the courage of their convictions. Brave

action always follows courageous commitment. "Where have all
the heroes gone?" was a theme song of the past decade. I definitely believe that the heroes of the faith found in the actions of
God's Holy Spirit are marshaling again around the world to boldly
and bravely claim our day for his honor and glory.

These two words—*commitment* and *courage*—epitomize the
lives of these heroes of the faith in the book of Acts. Peter and
John were taken before the Sanhedrin and questioned about their
commitment to Jesus Christ. They were actually standing before
the supreme court of the Jews. The supreme court (or Sanhedrin)
had seventy-one members. Peter, the Galilean fisherman, stood
before the court and took the occasion to courageously and eloquently point them to Jesus Christ. He was speaking to a group
that represented the wealthiest, the most intellectual, and the most
powerful people in his country. He declared, "This is the stone
which was rejected by you builders, but which has become the
head of the corner. And there is salvation in no one else, for there
is no other name under heaven given among men by which we
must be saved" (Acts 4:11-12, RSV).

We have enough professing Christians today in our churches
across America to actually share the message of Christ with every
American citizen within a matter of days, if we would but do it.
Instead, we are plagued by a lack of Christian courage today.
Creeping cowardice plagues us and withholds the results of real
revival in our midst! Peter, guided by the Holy Spirit, said to
them, "It is by the authority of Jesus Christ." God certified their
courage. He actually endorsed them authoritatively to courageously do his work.

The Holy Spirit Captured Their Bold Concentration

Too often we preach commitment and call for courage, but we
do it without a spiritual pattern. These disciples actually changed
their pattern of living. That is bold concentration. The pattern of
their living was the result of that bold concentration on the things
of God. This pattern change is not optional. It is a part of the difference. Here is a part of their concentrated pattern change spelled
out! "They gave themselves to each other." They began to love

each other. No more of the typical knifing each other in the back. They studied the Bible and prayed together. They concentrated, they dug in; they persisted in Bible study and prayer.

The apostle Paul revealed this when he said to the church at Philippi, "My brothers, I do not consider myself to have fully grasped it even now. But I do concentrate on this: I forget all that lies behind me and with hands outstretched to whatever lies ahead I go straight for the goal—my reward the honour of my high calling by God in Christ Jesus" (Phil. 3:12-14, Phillips). The apostle understood motivation. He knew that he must have a personal spiritual goals program, and he prayerfully went "straight for the goal." He actually concentrated on nothing else!

The power of bold concentration on the things of Jesus Christ is beginning to spark fires of revival throughout the world. Jesus taught us that ultimately a man will become what he thinks about. That is why he said, "Every man who looks at a woman lustfully has already committed adultery with her—in his heart" (Matt. 5:28, Phillips), and 1 John 3:15 states, "The man who hates his brother is at heart a murderer" (Phillips). The Master Teacher reveals a psychological truism that is still in operation today. Lust is the seed of adultery. Plant the seed and it will grow. Hatred is the seed of murder. Plant the seed and it will grow from hate to the overt act of murder if left unchecked. Therefore, whatever we concentrate on (habitually think about) will be planted in our subconscious mind and ultimately will bear fruit. That is why the apostle Paul preached so much and urged "think on these things." He stood before Governor Felix and his wife Drusilla and said, "I want you to reason (concentrate) on what it means to be rightly related (righteous) to God on a personal level" (Acts 24:25, author's translation). Paul knew that attitude was really a habit of thought. What you think about and concentrate on will ultimately surface as your attitude about life. He urged the Christians at Philippi to, "Let your attitude to life be that of Jesus Christ himself" (Phil. 2:5, Phillips).

Bold spiritual concentration is the wellspring of creative imagination. The mathematical genius Albert Einstein said, "Imagination is more important than knowledge." In the Old Testament, prior to the flood, we read that God condemned the people for evil imaginations. "And God saw that the wickedness of man was great in the earth, and that every imagination of the thoughts of his heart was only evil continually" (Gen. 6:5). So gross was this in God's sight that it "grieved him at his heart" (Gen. 6:6). God speaks of the thoughts of man's heart producing evil imaginations. Concentration feeds imagination. Imagination can conquer. Therefore concentrate (think) on the bold admonition of our Lord and the result will be creative Christian imagination.

The Aluminum Company of America received credit for coining the word *imagineering.* Imagineering means that "you let your imagination soar and then engineer it down to earth. You think about the things you used to make, and decide that if you don't find out some way to make them immediately better, you may never be asked by your customers to make them again." Can you see the Christian corollation? Whatever we boldly concentrate on ultimately expresses itself in our imagination. We use our energies to engineer our dreams into realities. We will boldly concentrate on his Great Commission when we are captured by his Spirit!

Enthusiasm is the result of bold concentration. The Greeks gave us the word *enthusiasm* with its true meaning found in *en theos.* Actually, "in God," or "God in you." We, of all people, should be the most enthusiastic in our quest to share God's love.

The most enthusiastic people I know are those who courageously live for Christ. Their basic commitment has changed their bold concentration so that God can move through them to accomplish his will today!

Basic commitment . . . brave courage . . . bold concentration. These are powerful words, and they are the scriptural keys to being captured by God's Spirit! Man has a long history of prostituting power. This is true spiritually as well as politically and economically. God has given himself to us! At Calvary, for the remission of sins. But God expressed at Pentecost that he is still giving of himself in power to us through his Spirit.

Draw a triangle in your mind. Put the name of God in the center of the triangle. At the top write *Father,* and at the two points at the bottom write *Son* and *Holy Spirit.* It is an equilateral triangle:

God: the Father; God: the Son; and God: the Holy Spirit. God is our power! Without him all ultimately fails.

We need to pray the prayer, "I pray, not what I want but what you want" (Matt. 26:39, Williams). I commit! I entrust my all to thee! I want to have your courage as I concentrate on doing your will in my life, in my world!" And we will be captured by his Spirit. He has promised, and he always keeps his promises!

Note

[1]William Barclay, *The Daily Study Bible, The Acts of the Apostles* (Philadelphia: The Westminster Press, 1955), p. 36.

Duke K. McCall has served as the president of Southern Baptist Theological Seminary, Louisville, Kentucky, since 1951. He is a native of Meridian, Mississippi, and a graduate of Southern Baptist Theological Seminary.

5
GOD'S UNDERSHEPHERD

Acts 20:17-32

Paul's farewell to the beloved church at Ephesus gives a vivid description of his own role as a Christian minister. In the midst of this emotionally charged, impassioned farewell he turned to his fellow ministers and said, "Take heed therefore unto yourselves, and to all the flock, over the which the Holy Ghost hath made you overseers, to feed the church of God, which he hath purchased with his own blood" (v. 28).

Every pastor is God's undershepherd. Consideration of the

word *undershepherd* produces three questions. What is he under? What is he over? What is he for?

The undershepherd is under God because he was adopted by the God and Father of our Lord Jesus Christ. God has called him with the high calling to be a Christian (see Phil. 3:14). This is the basic element in the making of any pastor. He is called under the lordship of Christ to be washed in the blood and redeemed and transformed. "Old things are passed away; behold, all things are become new" (2 Cor. 5:17). He is a new creation in Christ because of his call to be a Christian.

But he is under God because he was called to be a minister of the gospel of Jesus Christ. This call has its secret dimension and its ecclesiastical dimension. There is no one who can fully describe the inner or secret call by which a Christian feels himself compelled in the providence, grace, and mercy of God to become a minister, a pastor. The public side of the secret call is the action of the people of God in a church which sets him apart by ordination and by the invitation to be their undershepherd.

But if we talk about his call, we must talk about who calls him. He is called by the God who created the heavens and the earth, who piled the hills upon the hills to create the mountains, who strung the stars in the sky, who hollowed out the caverns of the deep. It is he who, "in the beginning . . . created the heaven and the earth. And the earth was without form, and void; and darkness was upon the face of the deep. And the spirit of God moved upon the face of the waters. And God said, Let there be light: and there was light" (Gen. 1:1-3).

God's undershepherd has made an ultimate, final faith commitment to believe in God. He lives under the authority, guidance, and protection of God.

Some years ago I traveled by train to a preaching engagement in Dallas, Texas. In the old Pullman I was working on my sermon— my books scattered about on a table in front of me. The man across the aisle got tired of looking out the window at the sweeping Texas plains. In Texas you can see farther and see less than anywhere else in the world. And he had already seen it. So he slipped across the aisle and sat opposite me. He picked up my Bible and looked at it quizzically. Finally he said, "This is a Bible?" Now that did not seem to be a very intelligent thing because it clearly said right on the spine "Bible." Then he added, "I don't believe a word of it." I resisted the almost overpowering impulse to suggest that he quietly get lost and let me finish my work. But that did not sound like something appropriate for a Baptist preacher to say. Instead I said, "What do you believe?"

He said, with obvious pride, "I am an agnostic."

"What," I asked, "do you mean by 'agnostic?' "

"Well," he said, "agnostic is a Greek word. A at the beginning reverses the meaning in Greek, and a *gnostic* is a knower; so I am a man who is simply honest enough to admit that I do not know whether there is a God or not."

Frankly, I am good at giving a witty reply with only one small defect. I think of the smart answer just twenty-four hours too late to use it. But that time I think the Holy Spirit gave me an answer. I said, "I do not use the Greek very often. I always use the Latin."

He bit. "What," he said, "is the Latin equivalent of 'agnostic?' "

I said, "The Latin equivalent is *ignoramus*." Can you imagine anyone boastfully claiming to be an *ignoramus*?

According to the psalmist, "The fool hath said in his heart, There is no God" (Ps. 14:1). For the wise man, "the heavens declare the glory of God; and the firmament showeth his handiwork" (Ps. 19:1).

God is. God is the great affirmation of faith of the Christian minister. And because he has made that faith commitment, the whole world is different.

In Browning's poem, "Pippa Passes," the little girl, Pippa, on her one holiday in the year sings a happy song:

> The year's at the spring
> and day's at the morn;
> morning at seven;
> the hill-sides dew pearled;
> the lark's on the wing;
> the snail's on the thorn;
> God's in his heaven—
> all's right with the world!

During World War II a chapel speaker at the New Orleans Seminary quoted the last line and said, "Anyone who has read the morning newspaper knows that all is not right with the world." After chapel as we sat in the president's office drinking the inevitable cup of New Orleans coffee, and I said to the speaker, "Did you know you misquoted Browning?"

"How is that?" he replied.

I said, "It was the little girl who went out that happy holiday singing her song. Behind shadowed windows Ottima and her German lover, Sebald, were awakening to a dark and dreary day, bitter with a debauched and illicit love affair which had led them to murder Ottima's husband. For them, all was wrong with the world. But for the little girl, Pippa, she had a basic premise—'God is in his heaven,' so for her 'all's right with the world.' "

One of the characteristics of God's undershepherd is that, in the awesome tides and turbulent times in which we live, when political structures crumble and economic systems collapse and social systems are in disarray, he is not pessimistic; he is not downcast; he is not discouraged—for him, God is in heaven and all is right with the world. There is an optimism based not on confidence, not in human frailty, but in the providence and purpose of almighty God.

As God's undershepherd, it is not his business to carry the weight of the whole world on his back. It is not even his business to straighten out all the wrongs in the world or in anywise bear the whole burden of humanity. It is his burden to do what God has called him to do. Therefore, when he has faithfully served the God who commissioned, called, and ordained him, he can expect to hear at the close of the race of life, "Well done, thou good and faithful servant" (Matt. 25:21). He is not responsible for the outcome, for that is in God's hands. But he is responsible for the faithful proclamation of the gospel of God's Son, Jesus Christ our Lord and Savior.

The effectiveness of the work of the undershepherd is guaranteed by what God has done in the incarnation, whereby the "word was made flesh, and dwelt among us" (John 1:14). It is because God purposed to redeem the lost that he "gave his only begotten Son, that whosoever believeth in him should not perish, but have everlasting life" (John 3:16). This is the irresistable, triumphant work of God; and therefore, the success of God's work on earth, the extension of God's kingdom, is not up to the undershepherd. Rather it is up to the undershepherd to believe in God, to accept his redeeming grace, and to proclaim the Holy Spirit's power as evidenced in the good news of what God has already done.

Thus, because he is under God, the undershepherd is a man under orders. Because he is under God, he is filled with the grace and mercy of God. Because he is under God, he is the instrument of the most powerful force in the universe—the redemptive love of God.

Overseer

The pastor is not only undershepherd for God but he is also the overseer of the church of God. Often in the New Testament, the pastor is referred to as a bishop (see Phil. 1:1; 1 Tim. 3:1; Titus 1:7). But when the term *bishop* is put into plain English, it simply means that he is the "overseer of the church."

We Baptists do not like the term *bishop*. We don't use it because it has come to mean, in the usage of other churches, a high-ranking church official. We prefer to talk about the priesthood of believers and then derive the democracy of the saints from the priesthood of believers. Unfortunately, the political model of democracy to be found throughout our land has come to dominate our idea of the decision-making process in the church. This precludes the understanding of the pastor as the spiritual overseer of the body of Christ. We need to turn our thoughts away from the Republican and Democratic parties and stop looking at city, state, or federal government and focus our attention on the biblical revelation. The result would be a way of understanding the church which would make clear that the pastor is indeed an overseer.

A Christian church is neither "my church" nor "our church." It is "Christ's church." When Jesus said, "Upon this rock I will build my church," the disciples knew what "church" meant; but the new ingredient was "my." What did that personal pronoun add to the congregation or assembly of the people of God?

Let me share with you the experience that brought home to me this new ingredient in the church. I was pastor of a small, halftime country church in west Tennessee. The grapevine had brought me the news that the pulpit committee from the nearby county seat was coming to hear me preach on the next Sunday. I was in my room at my parents' home in Memphis, Tennessee, working hard to get an impressive sermon ready for the pulpit committee.

My lawyer father, a deacon in his church, came into my room. "I hear you are going to have important company in your church this Sunday," he said. I was surprised. How did he as a layman know about the pulpit committee?

"Who told you the pulpit committee was coming?" I asked.

"Oh, I was not talking about a pulpit committee," he said. "I was talking about somebody really important."

Who could be more important to a young pastor just beginning his ministry in a small church? "Who are you talking about?" I asked expectantly.

"You don't know?" he said with surprise in his voice. "Why, I thought that Jesus promised that 'where two or three are gathered together in his name, there he would be in the midst of them,' and you are not expecting him to be present in your church this Sunday morning?" Without waiting for an answer, because he knew he had embarrassed me terribly, he turned and left the room.

I closed the door behind him and got down on my knees to pray, "Oh, God, never let me go into any church anywhere, anytime without expecting Jesus to be present in his church in miracle-working power." Without the presence of Christ, no gathering in any building is a Christian church!

The characteristic of a genuinely Christian church is that it is Christ's church. He is the head of it. The democratic process for decision making is simply a way to let all of the saints express what each one believes to be *the mind of Christ* in the matter to be decided. In a truly Christian church, no member votes his or her personal desire or private opinion or personal preference. That is the understanding of the church as a democracy which issues in disagreement and division and hurt feelings. But unity and power and progress come out of the democratic process when each Christian votes what he believes Jesus Christ would want his church to do in that situation.

Obviously, no church ever hires a preacher when it is acting out what it believes to be the mind of Christ. It calls the man of God to minister in that church. It looks not for a young man or an old man, a go-getter, or an eloquent preacher. It seeks God's undershepherd to be the overseer of the spiritual life of that congregation. He is a man to be loved and respected, to be cherished and honored because he has been called of God as an undershepherd and because in his daily life he represents and is characterized by spiritual concern.

The ministry of the laity is a New Testament teaching. However, where churches have become spiritually powerful and evangelistically effective, the ministry of the laity is carried on under the overseer of the church, God's undershepherd.

The man who is not worthy to be God's undershepherd ought to get out of the ministry. The church which does not want to function under God's overseer ought to quit calling itself Christian. The role of undershepherd, is one no pastor can claim and require for himself. The role of overseer is the gift of the church and should be implicit in the call of a pastor. And that role will be bestowed upon the pastor if the church is indeed functioning under the lordship of Christ trying to know and express the mind of Christ rather than the majority opinion of its members. Every year every pastor should remind the members of a Christian church who they are and who he is. Then together the church and the pastor should examine the degree to which they are filling out the New Testament model of a church.

The Shepherd

If the pastor is under God and an overseer of the people of God, he will function as the shepherd of souls.

Jesus described himself as the "Good Shepherd" (see John 10:14). More than once he described the selfless concern of the Good Shepherd for the welfare of the sheep. It is obvious that the pastor must tend the flock of the people of God, binding up their hurts, guiding them in the "green pastures, by the still waters," protecting them against the powers of evil loose in our demonic world.

But the most poignant, powerful, persuasive picture of the work of the shepherd is in the parable Jesus told about the ninety-nine sheep safe in the fold. But one sheep was lost. The shepherd could not rest. The shepherd could not rejoice in the safety of the ninety and nine. The shepherd could not give himself to repairing the sheepfold. The shepherd could not go home to his family saying, "I will have to get up early tomorrow and look for the sheep that is lost." Immediately and urgently, even in the darkness of the night, he must go out to look and look until he finds the one sheep that was lost (Luke 15:3-7).

The work of God's undershepherd is never done. While there is one lost man or woman, boy or girl anywhere in the world, he must organize the manhunt by the people of God. He must lead them in their determination to find some way to recover the lost sheep of God's flock.

It is for this reason that the people of God who cooperate within the fellowship of the Southern Baptist Convention have purposed to be on Bold Mission.

Not just one pastor or one church, but all the people of God unite in an extraordinary effort to proclaim the gospel to every individual between now and the turn of the century.

They are not doing business as usual, but heroically committing time, energy, and money to the meeting of human needs in the name of the Christ who considers a cup of cold water in his name an important gift.

Already we are late in beginning because the boldest act for the sake of mankind was the incarnation, God's Son refusing to grasp or hold on to the glory of heaven which was his right. Instead he came and suffered death, even the death of the cross to turn the world back toward God, its Maker.

The task is too big for any one of us to do alone. It is too big for any one church to do alone. It is too big for the churches in an association to complete the job. It is too big for a state convention or even the Southern Baptist Convention to finish the task. But it is not too big for us together, as laborers together with God to bring the kingdoms of this world to become the kingdom of our Lord and of his Christ, that he may reign forever and forever.

James H. Smith has served as the Executive Director-Treasurer of the Brotherhood Commission of the Southern Baptist Convention since September, 1979. He is a native of Somerville, Alabama, and is a graduate of Central Baptist Seminary.

6
MOBILIZING MEN FOR MISSION MINISTRIES

Isaiah 6:1-9

King Uzziah was dead. For fifty-two years good King Uzziah had ruled Judah in peace and prosperity. But now he was dead. For ten years the northern kingdom, Israel, had been under the threat of invasion from the Assyrians. Annually, they had paid a great price to buy temporary peace. The fierce, war-loving Assyrians had threatened Judah. Uzziah had been successful in staying the enemy. Peace and prosperity had prevailed.

The years of luxury and leisure had lulled the people into moral and spiritual apathy. Things and thrills had become more important than God and righteousness. Now, King Uzziah was dead, and the outlook was dark. The future was uncertain; the people were afraid. Would young Jotham be able to seize the reins of government and lead them into the future as his father had done?

Someone once said, "When the outlook is dark, try the uplook." This was exactly what Isaiah did when he went up to the house of the Lord. And it was there in the midst of his despair, in the light of the uncertainty of the future, gripped by fear and doubt, he had an experience that literally changed his whole life.

There is a message in this story for America. We are living in times similar to those which faced Judah at the death of King Uzziah. Economically we face troubled times. Politically there is confusion; there is no certain voice. Morally and spiritually there is apathy and indifference. People are living in fear. There is serious doubt about the future. Prophets are already predicting the destruction of America as we know it. The outlook is indeed dark, and it is time to try the uplook.

A Vision

When Isaiah went up to the house of the Lord, "he saw the Lord." He had a vision. The writer of Proverbs said, "Where there is no vision, the people perish" (Prov. 29:18).

The problem with most people today is that they have no vision. Many pastors have no vision for themselves or for their churches. The majority of people have no vision. In fact, aimlessness is one of the primary characteristics of our time. People are not thinking about the future, and they are not making plans for it. About all that they are looking for as someone has said is "quittin' time and payday."

Leonard W. Sapp, a very successful commercial realtor in Springfield, Illinois, has the slogan for his operation, "We specialize in imagineering." Pastors who specialize in imagineering are building great churches. Laymen who are specializing in imagineering are finding significant meaning in their lives and many exciting outlooks for their Christian commitment.

In Acts 2:16-17, Simon Peter, filled with the Holy Spirit on the day of Pentecost, made reference to Joel 2:28 when he stated, "Your young men shall see visions, and your old men shall dream dreams." We are told that a dream is based upon a past experience. A vision is based upon a present situation and a future possibility. It is somewhat significant that it is the old men (not in years but attitude) who dream dreams; it is the young men who see visions.

The observation has been made that when a person continues to talk about the "good ole days," it is a sign that they are getting old. Very frankly, I have no desire to go back to the "good ole days." I remember very distinctly my own boyhood. Our house had four rooms and a path. The only running water was when we ran out to the well, drew a bucket out of the well using the rope and pulley, and then ran back into the house. Very frankly, I have no desire to go back to that kind of a situation. There are serious doubts about how good the "good ole days" really were.

Dr. Walter Pope Binns was president of William Jewel College in Liberty, Missouri, for nineteen years. One Sunday morning I heard him delivering the baccalaureate sermon to a graduating class. He made reference to a portion of Scripture that, very frankly, I had never seen before. It is found in 1 Chronicles 11. It is the story of Benaiah, the son of Jehoiada. It states that Benaiah was a great man and was numbered with the top thirty in the cabinet of King David (v. 25). But it also states very precisely that he did not attain to the greatness of the top three even though he "slew a lion in a pit in a snowy day" (v. 22).

Dr. Binns said the story had puzzled him for a number of years. Benaiah's failure to attain to the greatness that he might have attained was definitely related to the fact that he had slain a lion in the midst of a pit in the time of snow, even though he was a man of courage and mighty deeds. And then he said, "Just this past week, I saw it for the first time." He went ahead to explain what he thought had happened to a man who had done a courageous thing. Benaiah had gone down into a pit on a wintery day and maybe barehanded, slayed a mountain lion, but he never got over that experience as long as he lived. When Benaiah met the boys down at the city gates, he would open the conversation by saying, "I'd like to tell you fellows about the time I slew a lion in the midst of a pit in the time of snow." For the rest of his life, every time he met a new friend he would say, "By the way, did you hear about the time that I slew a lion in the midst of a pit in the time of snow?"

Many people never get over having had one successful achievement. There are pastors today who still talk about the revival they had forty years ago. Others remind you of the time they went out on a mission tour, but that was twenty years ago. There are those who assure you that God answers prayer because he answered their prayers—fifteen years ago. And some continue to tell you about the time they won someone to Jesus Christ, a quarter of a century ago. They continue to look back; they dream dreams. "Where there is no vision, the people perish" (Prov. 29:18).

Jesus said, "No man, having put his hand to the plough, and looking back, is fit for the kingdom of God" (Luke 9:62).

A Vision of God

The vision of Isaiah was threefold. It started with a vision of God, "I saw the Lord." Renewal begins with a vision of God. We must see God as he is. This is the day of deifying man and humanizing God. God is often referred to as, "the man upstairs," or "ole buddy."

Recently, I heard a Nashville crooner singing on the radio, "Just me and God" and most of the emphasis was upon "me."

Isaiah saw the Lord in his absolute holiness. It was not that God is holier than man, God is absolute holiness and in him there is no unholiness. God is righteous, and in him there is no unrighteousness.

A Vision of Self

In the light of the splendor of the glory of God, Isaiah saw himself as he really was, "Woe is me! for I am undone; because I am a man of unclean lips" (Isa. 6:5). Isaiah saw that his dirty mouth was nothing more than the expression of the dirt that was in his soul.

If we compare ourselves to other people, we get an exhalted opinion. It's easy to find someone whom we consider worse than we are. We do not see ourselves as we really are until we see ourselves against the absolute righteousness of God.

When Charles Hadden Spurgeon was pastor in London, one bleak winter day he went to visit a member of his congregation who was dying. As he stepped upon the porch, he noticed the laundry that had been freshly done hanging on the line. Against the dreary background of a winter day in London, it looked sparkling white. He commented about how clean and fresh it looked. The lady who greeted him at the door had done the laundry and received his compliment with pride. Shortly after the pastor had entered the house, a winter snow began to fall and it fell for quite some time as he extended his visit. Upon leaving, the same laundry was hanging on the same line, but against a different background. Now instead of looking sparkling white, it showed signs of tattletale gray. In fact, it was so dingy, it almost looked dirty. He didn't say a word, but the lady who had received the compliment only a short time before, could not contain her embarassment and spoke out saying, "Who can compete with the whiteness of God?"

When we see God as he really is and when we see ourselves as we really are, we are apt to be like the publican in the story told by Jesus. His response was, "God be merciful to me a sinner" (Luke 18:13).

A Vision of Those About Us

When Isaiah had seen himself as he was, in light of who God was, he was able to see those about him more clearly. "I dwell in the midst of a people of unclean lips" (Isa. 6:5). He recognized that the people about him were having the same problems that he was having. They were basically what he was. After he experienced forgiveness and cleansing for his own sins, he desired forgiveness and cleansing for them.

In order to minister to our world, we must see those about us as they are. Recently, in a group of denominational leaders, I heard a report on the trends of our times. A specialist indicated that there is a dramatic, frightening, significant increase in stress in our society. The focal point is the economic uncertainty in our society. There is a new focus on "the me; the self; on what I want; what I need; what I desire." The next decade may well be known as the "Me Decade."

The trends of our time are for self-fulfillment, self-assertion, self-achievement, self-entitlement. There is a growing attitude that "I deserve it." The commercial advertising media is already picking up on it. "Sure it costs more, but I'm worth it." In order to minister to those about us, we must see them as they really are.

A Voice

In addition to seeing a vision, Isaiah heard a voice. The Lord said, "Whom shall I send, and who will go for us" (v. 8)? In our world there are many voices. They sound like hawkers at a visiting carnival. "Come see my show." "Come buy my wares." There are voices, voices, voices everywhere. Some are persuasive, some are demanding, some are challenging, some are threatening, some are exciting, some are seductive. Most promise more than they can deliver. The voice of pleasure is a dominant voice today. "Did you have fun?" "If it feels good, do it." "Go ahead, do as you please."

The Bible states that, "in the last days . . . men will be lovers of pleasure more than lovers of God" (2 Tim. 3:1, 4). Paul observed that "she that liveth in pleasure is dead while she liveth" (1 Tim. 5:6). God declares that it is better "to suffer affliction . . . than to enjoy the pleasures of sin for a season" (Heb. 11:25). They do not satisfy; they are merely passing away. Yet in the midst of all the clamor, there is a still, small voice. "Whom shall I send, and who will go for us" (Isa. 6:8). God's still calling. The call of God is to salvation. The call of God is to service. God is calling young people into vocational Christian service in unprecedented numbers. God is calling lay persons to give a part of their time in vocational skills to mission ministries. God is calling healthy, economically secure people to retire early and give some of their best years on a field of missions. The voice of God may be heard through the invitation of a pastor. It may be through a mission journal or personal visit to an area of need. God is still saying, "Whom shall I send, who will go for us?"

A Volunteer

A vision and voice led Isaiah to say, "Here am I, Lord, send me" (6:8). He was a volunteer. Response to God's call is always on a volunteer basis. The call of Jesus to his disciples was a simple "Follow me." Those who responded were volunteers. God's army has always been made up of volunteers. Jesus said, "If any man will come after me, let him deny himself, and take up his cross, and follow me" (Matt. 16:24).

The decade of the 1980s will be known as the "The Decade of the Laity." It will be a decade of volunteer ministers. Every believer in Jesus Christ is called to serve, that is to minister. Everyone is a minister. Not all have been called to preach or to teach, but all have been called to minister. It is impossible to hire enough paid professionals to evangelize the world. It was never God's plan that the world would be evangelized by a select group of paid professionals. Many sincere, dedicated men are rethinking their priorities. They are coming to the decision to work enough to provide an adequate livelihood for their families, then volunteer their time and professional expertise to mission ministries.

Recently, 650 Baptist men volunteered to form a clean-up operation in a Southern city that had been devastated by a hurricane. They came from five states, paying their own expenses. On Sunday morning they arrived with chain saws to remove trees and limbs and other debris. Others moved in with hot food and clean water units. It was not just a humanitarian act performed by a service club, it was a mission ministry in the name of Jesus. They served and gave witness to their faith in Jesus Christ.

Several state conventions have purchased disaster relief units, and the Brotherhood Departments have trained teams of volunteers to move on a moment's notice. In the wake of a disaster, there are desperate needs for doctors, first-aid assistants, carpenters, electricians, and men who are willing to do hard work of clearing debris.

In the rendering of professional service, the door is wide open for them to bear witness of their faith in Jesus Christ and, therefore, turn what could be merely humanitarian into a mission ministry.

Recently, I visited the executive director of a northern state convention. He took me to a building site in his city. The state Brotherhood director and twenty-six other men were building a church house. It started on a concrete slab on Monday morning. Their goal was to have it finished by Sunday so the congregation could worship. They achieved that goal, including completing the baptistry, which was used the opening Sunday. These men were all volunteers. They not only had left their jobs for the week but they also paid their own expenses while giving their professional skills for the week. The cost of that church to the congregation was only the cost of materials. The ministry rendered by these men put that congregation literally years ahead in their progress in ministering to the community where they were. The interesting thing, however, was that this church was the eighth one built in that one summer by that state Brotherhood Department.

Several state conventions have organizations of "Carpenters for Christ" or "Builders for Christ." Most of these have started by an interested Baptist layman who volunteered the time, and others joined him. They experienced something of the thrill of going out on a mission ministry.

In hearing the testimony from those who have had this type of experience, they declare that they will never let another year go by without going out again and again.

During the next few years, there will be a number of Baptist vocational, professional fellowships. There will be fellowships of Baptist men in medicine, Baptist men in dentistry, Baptist men in government, Baptist men in agriculture, Baptist men in business, Baptist men in management. There is no limit to the list. God is able to use every gift, every vocational skill that he has given. Will you be a volunteer?

"As a Volunteer"

A call for loyal soldiers Comes to one and all;
Soldiers for the conflict, Will you heed the call!

Will you answer quickly, With a ready cheer?
Will you be enlisted As a volunteer?
He calls you, for He loves you, With a heart most kind.
He whose heart was broken, Broken for mankind;
Now, just now He calls you, Calls in accents clear,
Will you be enlisted As a volunteer?

A volunteer for Jesus, A soldier true!
Others have enlisted, Why not you?
Jesus is the Captain, We will never fear;
Will you be enlisted As a volunteer?*

James L. Pleitz has served as the pastor of the Park Cities Baptist Church, Dallas, Texas, since October, 1977. He is a native of Jonesboro, Arkansas, and a graduate of Southern Baptist Theological Seminary.

7
EQUIPPING THE SAINTS

Ephesians 4:11-12

The disciples were perplexed. The crowds were excited; the rulers hostile. In this energized atmosphere, Jesus delivered a powerful soliloquy in which he stated succinctly the purpose of his existence on the earth. Luke is the only writer who recorded it for us. "I came to cast fire upon the earth; and would that it were already kindled! I have a baptism to be baptized with; and how I am constrained until it is accomplished!" (Luke 12:49-50, RSV).

It is not possible for us to know exactly how our Lord was using the metaphor of fire. In the Old Testament fire generally refers to something terrible. In his interpretation of the New Testament, Elton Trueblood points out, "The figure of fire reaches an affirmative climax in the account of Pentecost, the great new experience being so far removed from mildness that it required the use of the fire metaphor to make it clear." Recall Acts 2:3, "And there appeared to them tongues as of fire distributed and resting on each one of them" (RSV). F. F. Bruce believes this fire to be the burning enthusiasm in the believers which tends to promote the antagonism in the unbelievers. Augustine, using the metaphor our Lord used, portrayed the entire Christian enterprise as that in which one loving heart (the believer) sets another (the unbeliever) on fire.

With only slight paraphrasing, John 17:18 becomes a mini-report from our Lord to his Father regarding his progress on earth: "I have completed the work of revealing the Father; I have deposited this truth with men and now I send them into the world for the same purpose that you sent me into the world." So if Jesus' purpose was to cast fire, then our purpose is to cast fire. And that purpose is accomplished when the Father is revealed. He is perfectly revealed through the Son. Our task is simply to make Jesus known throughout the earth. But, what a task! The more difficult the task, the more challenging the equipping of people to meet the task.

Now we come to the topic of this message: Equipping the Saints. *Equipping* is a word with rich imagery. William Barclay points out that in the New Testament its use suggested: (1) setting a limb that had been dislocated, (2) developing certain parts of the body through exercise, (3) restoring a person to his rightful mind, or (4) fully furnishing someone for a given purpose. The fourth meaning best describes its use in this message.

Saints here will refer to those persons who have experienced salvation through a personal encounter with the Lord Jesus Christ. No distinction is intended between the "professional" saint and the "lay" saint. We are all saints called to be his disciples.

I believe that a primary task of the church is to equip the saint to continue to spread the fire that was cast upon the earth by the birth, ministry, teaching, and the baptism (death) of our Lord. It is an awesome task.

As sixty-five thousand rabid fans made their way into Texas Stadium to experience a battle between the Dallas Cowboys and the Los Angeles Rams, a group of Cowboys were gathered at the stadium for a time of worship and Bible study. It was my sheer delight to be chosen to deliver the "game plan" on that occasion. I became (almost jealously) aware that I was speaking to some of the best equipped men in the world to perform a special assignment. Their task is simply to win football games and their preparation is unreal.

Coach Tom Landry, the person primarily responsible to see that the Cowboys are equipped, radiated a quiet confidence that assured me that he and I shared the same awareness. *He should be confident*, I thought. *To accomplish the task of winning football games, he has at his disposal the limit allowed by law of the finest football players in the world.* They came to the Cowboys with remarkable skills: runners who can run, blockers who block, tackles who tackle, receivers who catch, quarterbacks who do it all. Add to this the finest pre-game message I've ever preached to the Cowboys. Victory was assured. Cowboys 30, L.A. Rams 6. Coach Landry must have been very pleased.

I'm a coach. That title appeals to me more than doctor, reverend, mister, or some others that might be uttered in secret. My team is called Park Cities Baptist Church of Dallas, Texas. The roster is made up of saints. I choose to ignore the rumors that there are some impostors on the roster.

Like the Cowboys, the players on our team have special abilities. These abilities were given by the Holy Spirit and are called spiritual gifts. Each member of the squad has at least one gift and many of them possess several. The gifts were given to strengthen the team and to help us accomplish the assigned task. "And He gave some as apostles, and some as prophets, and some as evangelists, and some as pastors and teachers, for the equipping of the saints for the work of service, to the building up of the body of Christ" (Eph. 4:11-12, NAS).

How about that? The Holy Spirit of God is one of the equippers of our team. The task becomes more possible. And the preceding list of special gifts is by no means complete or exhaustive. The Holy Spirit distributes the special gifts as he chooses. Though they may atrophy through misuse or no use, they are absolute and forever.

Many of us are privileged to share the duties of equipping with the Holy Spirit and under his guidance. As the pastor (a title I'll settle for since my team simply will not call me coach) of a church called to spread the fire across a great metroplex, I have a responsibility to lead in the equipping of the members. But the task is not mine alone.

In his controversial book *Call to Discipleship*, Juan Carlos Ortiz is less than complimentary of the pastor as an equipper. "The pastor is the cork in the church. Nobody can go out because the pastor is not perfecting the saints for the work of the ministry. Rather, he is preventing the saints from becoming ministers." God forbid that any pastor ever deserves this harmful criticism. It does remind me, however, that the pastor must be a facilitator, an enabler, encouraging his members to get on with the work at hand.

Michael Harper, in his book *Let My People Grow*, acknowledges these five commands from the Lord: Go to my people—speak to my people—care for my people—talk to my people—reach my people. From these he fashioned five slogans:

Let my people go—the apostolic functions of the church.
Let my people hear—the prophetic function of the church.
Let my people care—the pastoral function of the church.
Let my people know—the teaching function of the church.
Let my people grow—the evangelistic function of the church.

Ephesians 4:11-12 assures us that for each of the functions, some of the saints have been given corresponding gifts, special abilities. We simply must recognize these remarkable resources that are available to the church as it spreads the fire.

Jesus began his ministry with the call of Peter and Andrew and James and John to follow him—to be his disciples. Throughout his ministry on earth Christ was busy about the work of making disciples and, as it closed, he commanded those disciples to make other disciples from all nations. Clearly, our Lord devoted his life to teaching and training. As we seriously consider the task of equipping the saints, we need to learn from his example and methods. The first words spoken to those who would become his disciples formed an exciting invitation: "Follow me." In Christ's name we need to faithfully encourage the members of our churches to follow him.

On one occasion when Jesus was inviting men to follow him, two having decided to follow, asked him where he lived. Jesus extended another invitation: Come and see. They came and saw (John 1:37). It seems he was always issuing the most unusual and exciting invitations. Not only did they see where he lived but they also learned who he was and probably who *they* were. Remember that is was not until Peter told Jesus who he was (the Christ) that Jesus told Peter who he was (the Rock). And we'll never really know ourselves fully until we know him more completely.

The equipping process obviously requires teaching skills and it is exciting to see the work that is going on in our own Southern Baptist denomination to equip our teachers. An example is the Equipping Center concept and materials that are being developed by the Church Training Department of the Baptist Sunday School Board and released to the churches. They effectively meet training needs in areas of Christian doctrine, Christian growth, church and community, evangelism and missions, family life, and leadership training. Each Equipping Center is made up of modules (study packages) that employ a variety of learning approaches or methodology.

Educators confess their fascination with how Jesus went about teaching. In a very fine book, *Equipping the Disciples*, one of the contributors, Earl Kelly, discusses how Christ secured his listener's attention. He used symbols, imagery, and personal association. He used impressions, parables, Scriptures, problems, and just plain talk. No you-sit-still-while-I-instill approach was apparent in the methods repertoire of the Master Teacher who seemed to realize that discipleship is more caught than taught.

Arthur Criscoe, referring to modeling and association (two elements in the teaching learning process that are too often overlooked by secular and religious educators), has said, "The teacher must embody and demonstrate in his own life the attitudes, values, and concepts he would teach." Generosity is seldom taught by a selfish person. It is difficult for one to share the love of Christ if he is at the same time experiencing unresolved anger, hostility, or hate.

He also encourages the use of the twin concepts of activity and self-discovery and points out that when Jesus invited Simon to "push the boat out further to the deep water, and you and your partners let down your nets for a catch" (Luke 5:4, TEV), both activity and self-discovery were involved. Criscoe says that equipping should "guide as the student explores, discovers, responds to, and appropriate truth for himself."

"Of all Jesus' teaching tools (preaching, healing, parables, demonstration, discussion, ritual, drama, encounter, and interpretation) the parable, whether it was in an art form or an action form, or in his own modeling of behaviour, was the most effective." This quote is credited to Robert Dow and serves to remind us that as we look for methods of equipping, we simply have no better example to study than our Lord.

A pastor readily recognizes that Jesus was a superb pastor. Someone has said that Jesus' high-priestly prayer was his report to the Father of his pastoral ministry. And it is there that all the main functions of pastoral care are touched upon. Michael Harper points out these components and the Lord's response: (1) Feeding—"I have given unto them the words which thou gavest me" (John 17:8). (2) Guarding—"While I was with them in the world, I kept them in thy name: those that thou gavest me I have kept" (John 7:12). (3) Praying—"I pray not that thou shouldest take them out of the world, but that thou shouldest keep them from evil. Sanctify them through thy truth" (John 17:15,17). (4) Consecrating—"And for their sakes I sanctify myself, that they also might be sanctified through the truth" (John 17:19).

In the apostolic function, Jesus' example is seen in an oft quoted statement: "God only had the one Son and he was a missionary!"

In a very fine compilation of the writings of many outstanding people, edited by John Hendrix and Lloyd Householder, *Equipping the Disciples*, many aspects of the task of equipping people to do the work of the church are considered. There is a need to equip in the art of loving, in spiritual awareness, in self-awareness, in self-sacrifice, in witnessing. We need to equip for the now and for the future. And how about servanthood and faithfulness; shepherding and caring?

The task is really overwhelming. But God has given us so many resources with which to work. When a group of young people in a church where I was pastor decided to minister to a group of cerebral palsy children, they discovered a need for a bowling ramp that could be used for recreation. God placed a man in the fellowship who built what is now called a Bowling Booster and is used throughout the country to provide recreation opportunities for crippled persons.

It is remarkable how eager Christians are to identify with a real challenge. Too often they move out of the church to identify with a para-church organization not because of what is happening in the church but because of what is *not* happening in the church. Could it be that we who are leaders in the church have become so aware of the magnitude of the task that we doubt if it is really possible to accomplish it? Have we seen the challenge without seeing the corresponding resources with which to meet the challenge? It is my conviction that the same Christ who has called us to a task is eager and able to empower us to do it.

Brooks H. Wester has served as the pastor of the First Baptist Church, Hattiesburg, Mississippi, since 1967. He is a native of Elgin, Texas, and a graduate of Southern Baptist Theological Seminary.

8
BOLD PRAYING

Matthew 9:35-38

The people of Jesus Christ who call themselves Southern Baptists have responded to God's awesome challenge to "Go ye therefore, and teach all nations, baptizing them in the name of the Father, and of the Son, and of the Holy Ghost: Teaching them to observe all things whatsoever I have commanded you" (Matt. 28:19-20), by seeking to perfect methods and develop resources that will enable them to have met that challenge by the year A.D. 2000. One important part of the mobilization of the people and their resources in this Bold Mission Thrust is the urgent call to the churches to lead the members of every congregation to become involved in bold praying. All other parts of Bold Mission Thrust will be limited in implementation and circumscribed in effectiveness by the boldness of our prayers. If ever there was a time for walking with God in bold praying, that time is the decades remaining in the twentieth century.

One of the rewarding studies to be made in the biblical revelation is the prayer life of saints and sinners whose experiences of walking with God are recorded in the divinely inspired Scriptures. The Bible indicates that men did not call upon the name of the Lord until the birth of Enos to Seth, the third son of Adam and Eve (Gen. 4:26).

The Bible further records that the seventh generation of man witnessed a man who not only called upon the name of the Lord, but "Enoch walked with God: and he was not; for God took him" (Gen. 5:24). The New Testament commented on the life of that remarkable man when the author of the letter of the Hebrews wrote, "By faith Enoch was translated that he should not see death; and was not found, because God had translated him: for before his translation he had this testimony, that he pleased God" (Heb. 11:5).

The tenth generation of man produced a period of great wickedness. But in the midst of all the prevailing evil there lived a man who found favor in the eyes of the Lord. The Bible reports that, "Noah was a just man and perfect in his generations, and Noah walked with God" (Gen. 6:9).

The remaining pages of the Old Testament are filled with the accounts of people who walked with God, some in good and prosperous times, and some in evil and depressing days. People whose portraits were a blessing to all who beheld them. People whose accomplishments for God were always preceded with, and accompanied by, seasons of bold praying.

The New Testament is filled with records of the lives of people who were bold in prayer. Every writer in the New Testament reminds the reader of the place and importance of prayer in their lives. The apostle Paul urged the churches to commit every interest of the missionary cause to intercessory prayer.

The greatest picture in God's gallery of the praying ones is his Son, Jesus Christ. The student of the life of Christ is aware from the very first that Jesus was a man of prayer. Dr. W. O. Carver, the great teacher of missions at the Southern Baptist Theological Seminary, was faithful to the Word of God when in his book, *Missions in the Plan of the Ages,* he wrote, "We shall do well to make diligent study of the prayer life of our Lord. It is significant that the incidents of His birth and first years move in an atmosphere of devout communication with God."[1] Dr. Carver then proceeded with a brief accounting of the instances when Jesus was reported to have been in prayer. The conclusion of his observations was, "When the climax of His life came and He was meeting the cross, our Lord forever sanctified a place and an experience when He 'poured out His soul unto death' in the prayer of Gethsemane and was 'heard for His godly fear.' So He came to His cross in prayer, and continued to utter prayer until He gave His spirit into the Father's care."[2]

Jesus taught his disciples to pray as he set for them an example and as he gave them subjects about which they were to pray. Dr. W. T. Conner, the late professor and head of the School of Theology at Southwestern Baptist Theological Seminary, in his book *The Christ We Need* has a chapter on the subject of "Jesus as a Man of Prayer." He pointed out that prayer for Jesus was a matter of habit and of fixed purpose. In his prayer life, Jesus took time to pray and often went aside from the crowds, and even his closest associates, to find a quiet place to pray. Dr. Conner also reminded his readers that Jesus prepared for the great crises in his life with prayer. When Jesus had fed five thousand, they wanted to force him to be their king; but Jesus went up into a mountain to pray. Jesus was in prayer for an entire night before choosing the twelve apostles. Every reader of the New Testament is impressed by the prayer of Jesus in Gethsemane as "he made the final surrender of himself to God and went to the cross in obedience to that will."

Dr. Conner further pointed to the record of Jesus' praying in what could be called the high hours of his life, such as his baptism and the transfiguration. He closed by saying, "Our high hours will also be hours of prayer. Such hours do not mean exemption from temptation and trials. Jesus' temptation in the wilderness came on the heels of His baptism and He met the demoniac boy when He came down from the Mount of Transfiguration. But in such high hours of prayer we can get strength for the temptations and trials of life. Without high hours of fellowship with God, our hours of trial and work will mean drudgery and failure and our hours of temptation will mean disaster and ruin."[3]

One of the subjects about which he wanted his disciples to pray was the need for laborers in the harvest of his Father in heaven. Matthew 9:35-38 presents the setting for his urgent teaching of his disciples to pray for laborers as well as the words of instruction.

Jesus had been passing through the cities and towns teaching in the local synagogues, preaching the gospel of the kingdom, and healing the people with sickness and disease. As he went, he was impressed by the great multitudes of people who followed to hear his words and to feel his touch. The deepest springs of compassion flowed from his heart to their hurts "because they fainted, and were scattered abroad, as sheep having no shepherd" (Matt. 9:36). With his compassion so deeply stirred by what he saw, Jesus urged his disciples to involve themselves in bold praying to "the Lord of the harvest, that he will send forth labourers into his harvest" (v. 38).

Dr. John A. Broadus reminded his readers in his work on the Gospel of Matthew in *An American Commentary,* that all Christians should feel the same depth of compassion as the Lord felt as he looked out over the throngs of people following him in Galilee and that we should pray regularly and habitually for the Lord of the harvest to send forth laborers into his harvest. Dr. Broadus also pointed out that the words "send forth" always implied urgency, haste, constraint, or some such idea, and in this verse meant that the laborers should be sent out promptly, pushed into their work. They must be the Lord's laborers, not ours, called into the work, and urged to performance by the Lord of the harvest himself.

Jesus was urging his disciples to engage in bold praying. I believe he calls his followers to be bold in praying today. To be successful in growing into a life of bold praying will require our walking with God and seeing our world through the eyes of our Lord Jesus. Christians today need to look through the eyes of Jesus at the people now populating the earth. Then they will have compassion on these people and pray for them. The numbers that demographers use to report the population of the nations of the world are very sobering to any thoughtful Christian. We are told there are over four billion persons living on our planet. Christian missiologists report that about one billion of the four billion identify themselves as Christians. It becomes glaringly apparent that to look at our world through the eyes of Jesus is to see three-fourths of the people as fainting in the heat of life as they now must live. Who can question the fact that people are scattered abroad and living without a shepherd to protect them and guide them to the safety of home. The crowded refugee camps that dot the maps of the earth are screaming evidence of the shepherdless multitudes living in our century.

As we grow more intimate with our Lord, as we become more faithful in walking with him let us be bold in praying for the compassionate heart that will have eyes to see the world as he sees it.

The participants in the International Congress on World Evangelization held in Lausanne, Switzerland, in 1974 will long remember the testimony of one of the participants from Africa as he reported the result in his life as he grew more bold in praying for his native tribe. He said that he came from a tribe that was totally illiterate. Under God's guidance he became a Christian. He came out of his tribal settlement to get an education and to become moderately successful in his chosen profession. All the while he never forgot to pray for his people. Then, he began to grow in his prayer life to the point of asking God to send missionaries to the tribe. While praying one day, the Lord impressed upon him that he was the one to go. He had all kinds of excuses to offer as to why he shouldn't go, but God's impression stayed with him. One of his excuses was to say to the Lord that his people were unable to read or write and, therefore, they wouldn't understand his educated ways. God's answer was to reveal that while they couldn't read or write, they could memorize what they heard. The man became God's answer to his own bold praying for someone to be sent to his people. He did teach them portions of the Bible. He then said, "When I returned to my people eight years ago, there were none who knew our Lord Jesus Christ, now there are none who do not know him and believe he is their Savior." One man walking with God in bold praying made the difference between darkness and light, life and death, for the people in his own African tribe. Prayer can make a difference anywhere in the world when believers put it to the test.

When the disciples saw the people as a ripened field of grain ready for harvest, they realized they needed help in gathering the people for the kingdom. Therefore, in their walking with the Lord, they boldly prayed for him to send forth more laborers into his harvest. Their prayer was not to be a substitute for the labor they were to do, for they were to be reapers as well as praying men. But the work would not get done without prayer for more workers.

Southern Baptists must do some bold praying for personnel to be sent forth to witness to every person on earth that Jesus Christ is the Savior for all people. To double the number of persons in the career mission force is a modest estimate of the actual requirements. Yet, to do that will demand an acceleration in numbers of volunteers and appointments beyond anything previously experienced. Bold praying to the Lord of the harvest to "thrust forth" personnel is not optional, it is imperative.

We must not forget that God uses the prayers of the saved to reach the lost, and he honors the praying of his people for more workers by calling them out to work in his harvest.

Around the turn of the twentieth century Dr. R. A. Torrey was an evangelist and Bible teacher with international influence whose life story is a testimony of the power of prayer in conversion and commitment to ministry. He shared his experience of conversion in a tract printed by The Bible Institute Colportage Association of Chicago in 1900. The title of the tract is *How to Pray.* He said:

There are few converted in this world unless in connection with someone's prayers. I formerly thought that no human being had anything to do with my own conversion, for I was not converted in church or Sunday School, or in a personal conversation with anyone. I was awakened in the middle of the night and converted. As far as I can remember I had not the slightest thought of being converted, or of anything of that character, when I went to bed and fell asleep; but I was awakened in the middle of the night and converted, probably inside of five minutes. A few minutes before I was about as near eternal perdition as one gets. I had one foot over the brink and was trying to get the other one over. I say I thought no human being had anything to do with it, but I had forgotten my mother's prayers, and I afterward learned that one of my classmates had chosen me as one to pray for until I was saved.

Southern Baptist students and church members can be an important part of Bold Mission Thrust by involving themselves in bold praying for the conversion of their classmates and friends and for the Lord of the harvest to send forth some of them into the world to witness for Christ.

When Southern Baptists have walked with God, have seen the world through the compassionate eyes of Jesus, and have been bold in praying for additional personnel in the mission enterprise, the need for bold praying is not ended. The missionary personnel will require bold prayer support for the work to be effective that God commissions them to do. There is no human way to measure the spiritual power generated in the lives of God's servants by the prayer support of the churches. The apostle Paul was constantly requesting the churches to "Pray always . . . for me that utterance may be given unto me, that I may open my mouth boldly, to make known the mystery of the gospel" (Eph. 6:19).

The story is told of a wonderful work of grace in the old China Island Mission under the leadership of the fabled missionary Hudson Taylor. The number and character of the converts in one station had been far greater than at some others where there was a concentration of more personnel. The rich harvest of souls had been a mystery to Hudson Taylor until he made a visit to England. He met a man who had a very good amount of knowledge and understanding of the mission work in China. Mr. Taylor asked him how he knew so much. The man replied that the missionary at that particular station was a college classmate and had corresponded regularly. He told of how his missionary friend had sent names of inquirers and converts and that daily he had taken those people to God in prayer. At last Mr. Taylor had the secret of success in China—a praying man in England, praying definitely, praying daily, praying boldly for specific people in China.

Southern Baptist missionaries will be strengthened in the performance of their witnessing by the bold praying of people in the churches who develop and grow in walking daily with God. We need to pray for God to give us all, both the missionary sent and the missionary sender, the power to speak for Christ.

We can so speak when we are willing to learn the joy of walking with God in bold praying.

Notes

[1]W. O. Carver, *Missions In the Plan of the Ages* (Nashville, Tennessee: Broadman Press, 1951), p. 217.

[2]Ibid.

[3]W. T. Conner, *The Christ We Need* (Grand Rapids, Michigan: Zondervan Publishing House, 1938), p. 54.

Jim Henry has served as pastor of First Baptist Church, Orlando, Florida, since 1977. He is a native of Nashville, Tennessee, and a graduate of New Orleans Baptist Theological Seminary.

9
LESSONS JESUS TAUGHT ABOUT WITNESSING

John 4

Someone asked Lyman Beecher, perhaps the greatest of all the Beechers, "Mr. Beecher, you know a great many things. What do you count the greatest thing that a human being can be or do?"

Without hesitation, the famous pulpiteer replied: "The greatest thing is not that one shall be a scientist, as important as that is; not that one shall be a statesman, vastly important as that is; nor even that one shall be a theologian, immeasurably important as that is; but the greatest thing of all, is for one human being to bring another to Christ Jesus, the Savior."

The longer I pastor, the more sure I am that Lyman Beecher was right. Outside one's own growing love relationship with Jesus, nothing can bless us, deepen us, extend us, thrill us, and encourage us better than leading someone else to know our Lord as their Savior and Lord. When an individual and a church get that firmly entrenched as a priority, two things will break loose: the blessings of heaven and the hatred of hell. Since we are in a spiritual war, that should not surprise us. Yet, more Christians and churches are blind sided by this more than anything else.

Jesus, our Lord, gave us a marvelous picture of witnessing while he was here. The fourth chapter of John gives us a window into his personal witnessing, as well as displaying some truths pertinent to understanding God's awesome challenge to his children.

Note first, *the method of witnessing* in verses 1—5. The witness? The Lord! One on one is still the best method. Dr. George Truett once said, "The supreme method for winning the world to Christ is the personal method, bringing people to Christ one by one." There are other ways: radio, television, tracts, mass evangelism; but it seems the most effective is one-to-one. Jesus preached his greatest sermon to one man, and taught in the parable of the lost sheep (Luke 15:3-7) the value of one. Andrew found his brother; Philip left a revival to lead one seeker to Christ; and Paul and Silas won the Philippian jailer. Henry Clay Turnbull, who had a long and effective ministry, wrote toward the last of his life: "I can see more direct results of good through my individual efforts with individuals than through all my spoken words in religious assemblies, or my written words in periodicals and books. Reaching one person at a time is the best way of reaching all the world in time."

Notice *the urgency of Jesus* (v. 4). Jesus was Spirit-driven to share his message with a woman who desperately needed to get a new start with a new heart. Not many of us have reached the compassion level of Jesus for the lost or even of David Brainerd, pioneer missionary to the Indians of the eastern shores of America. He would often be so burdened for the lost that he would fall off his horse into the snow and pray for hours for his Indian friends. In the latter months of his life, he would turn the snow red from the coughing effects of his tubercular lungs. Oh, how shallow our urgency! There is much to blunt it today. A spreading universalism that says men don't need to be saved, that they are already saved, or that they will be saved. A joining-the-church evangelism, where people ooze into membership but not into the kingdom. A distorted theology that enunciates God's sovereignty so much that man's responsibility is obliterated. And a rampant materialism that says, "I have all I need today. I could care less about my soul and eternity." I pray for more of Jesus' urgency in my daily walk: "Help me, Lord. Help us Lord to see people through your heart!"

Jesus dealt with obstacles to witnessing just as we must. In verses 7 and 9 we see *Jesus dealing with hindrances.* He had to deal with several cultural, religious, and social hindrances of his day. She was a woman. She was a Samaritan (the untouchables!), and she was promiscuous! But that didn't stop Jesus from witnessing.

Today, we must deal with hindrances and overcome them if we're to reach our world by the year A.D. 2000. Let me list several hindrances we must deal with. First, we have forgotten man's true nature. The Bible clearly states that man is lost and separated from God. Look at God's description of man as he sees him. Man's head is sick (Isa. 1:5); his eyes are evil (Mark 7:22); his mouth is deceitful (Ps. 36:3); his tongue is poison (Jas. 3:8); his neck is stiff (Jer. 17:23); his ears are dull (Matt. 13:15); his feet are running to mischief (Prov. 6:18); and his bones are full of sin (Job 20:11)! In spite of all our education, affluence, government, programs, and schemes, murders are soaring, venereal disease is at epidemic proportion, divorces parallel marriages, white-collar crime is at an all-time high, abortions are soaring, suicides are rising, and mental breakdowns are raging. Man does not need reupholstering, he needs a fresh start!

Second, we have forgotten the consequences of sin. Not only in the here and now but also in the bye-and-bye. Man, without Christ, is doomed to an eternity in hell. "For the wages of sin is death" (Rom. 6:23). God minces no words. Without Christ, there is a payday someday.

Third, I believe many pastors and churches have not made evangelism a priority. The best is substituted for the good. Sheep are fed and fed. They become takers instead of givers. Any kind of deepening spiritual life that does not result in a growing sensitivity and ministry of witnessing has a fatal flaw. When I see churches with two or three thousand members baptizing thirty or forty people a year, it does not take the FBI to evaluate what is happening. That church is doing church work instead of the work of the church. That leadership responsibility is plainly the pastor's. The buck stops at his place! The pastor must preach and practice witnessing. He must lead the church in that direction. No other institution in the world has the mandate to witness except the church. If we fail to witness, who will?

In the twelfth year of my ministry, I found myself having the joy of leading people regularly to the Lord. But it was the earnest plea of a concerned layman who one day said, "Pastor, take me with you. Show me how." That launched me into equipping our laity to witness. Beginning with two men in the evening and two women in the mornings and doubling that every six months, soon dozens of people were proficient in sharing Jesus. As a result, baptisms began to multiply. In five years we went from baptizing 128 to 286. I will never pastor a church without instituting a perennial soul-winning program. I believe most people know the *why* of witnessing, but there is a rising scream from the pew, saying, "How?" Brothers, that is our privilege and responsibility. I figure Jesus spent three years getting eleven men ready, answering their why's and showing them how.

Verse 14 gives us *the message of life* to be shared. That seems so simple in a complex world, but it sure reaches man's basic need. The basic needs of men are ageless. Man lives in the burden of guilt, the fear of death, the horror of loneliness, and the anxiety of meaninglessness. So many are like the seventeen-year-old girl who called me at 2 A.M. from a phone booth on a busy thoroughfare. She told me she had a pistol in her hand and she was going to end her life. When I asked her why, she replied, "Because nobody really cares anymore . . . but if you will tell me that you care if I live, even though you don't know me, I won't do it. I just want to know that somebody cares." There are people like her everywhere. They may not say it as dramatically, but they're experiencing it just the same. We have the message. As simple as it may sound to some, the truth is, "Christ is the answer." He becomes "a well of water springing up into everlasting life" (4:14). If you drink of him, you live. If you don't, you die. That is a simple message, and it's a true one.

Jesus' witnessing interview concludes with the woman's acceptance of his offer of life. Verses 39-42 reflect *the blessing and results of the witness.* Although the Scripture does not say so at this point, I'm sure there was joy over this one sinner who repented. Notice the blessing in the woman's life! She became a witness. She became the beggar who found bread leading other beggars to the Bread of life! William James said that religion was either a dull habit or an acute fever. The Samaritan woman caught the fever and I don't believe she ever lost it! When Christians start maximizing God's majors and minimizing the minors, there will be holy joy in the assembly of the saints again! The inevitable will result where we live and where our churches are planted—"and many more believed" (v. 41).

I met him in Panama City. He was walking his dog along the beach with his transistor radio blaring and his eager eyes combing the sand for treasures. He spotted me at the end of the pier. I watched him approach and although my body and soul were tired from an exhausting day, I decided if he came to me I would share Jesus with him. He came right to me and struck up a conversation. Bright and winsome, he was a delight to talk to. When I asked him about the Lord, he told me he went to church some and thought about God a lot. As clearly as I could, I introduced him to the Savior God. He listened intently and when I asked him if he would like to become a child of God, he said he would. I led him in a prayer of confession, encouraged him to follow through with his commitment, and after a few more minutes of fellowship, he departed.

The next day as our bus was ready to leave the campground, there was a knock on the door. The driver opened the door and there stood my friend from yesterday with a wrinkled brown bag in his hand. He shook my hand, jumped on his bike and followed our bus as long as his short legs could keep up. Then a last wave and he turned away. Curiously, I opened the bag. Inside, was the cork end of a fishing rod, a small toy flute, and a Charlie Brown funny book—I figured they were his favorite toys. As tears moistened my face, I realized they were a gift to me, to say "thanks for being my friend and telling me about Jesus." That's part of the blessing. Get in on it!

It is an awesome challenge, but so is life. When we make witnessing a priority in our personal life and in the place of responsibility the Lord has entrusted us, we will have a radical pulpit and a changed pew. Glory!

H. Franklin Paschall has been pastor of First Baptist Church, Nashville, Tennessee, since 1956. He was president of the Southern Baptist Convention from 1966-1968. He is a native of Hazel, Kentucky, and a graduate of Southern Baptist Theological Seminary.

10
THE CHRISTIAN PRESENTER

Romans 12:1

The Academy Awards program on television is watched by millions and is of some interest to all. One of the most important performers on this show is the presenter. He announces the nominees in a particular category of competition and then presents the person or persons who win the awards. This format is followed in many less prestigious events across the country as persons and products are presented for recognition and awards. In all these programs people and awards are presented to people.

There is another presentation which is far more significant. It is the Christian who presents himself to God. Paul said, "I beseech you therefore, brethren, by the mercies of God, that you present your bodies a living sacrifice, holy, acceptable unto God, which is your reasonable service" (Rom. 12:1).

The word *present* means "to place along side." It carries the idea of worship and refers to the proper placement of the sacrifice. In this verse the verb *present* is in the aorist tense which means a definite, deliberate and decisive act of commitment.

Worship and giving are inseparably related. The psalmist said, "Give unto the Lord the glory due unto his name: bring an offering, and come into his courts" (Ps. 96:8). He had in mind worship in the house of God, but worship can and should be continual, everyday, everywhere. Worship in God's house is special and the Bible teaches that at this place we are to bring a special measure of giving to God. "Bring ye all the tithes into the storehouse, that there may be meat in mine house, and prove me now herewith, saith the Lord of hosts, if I will not open you the windows of heaven, and pour you out a blessing, that there shall not be room enough to receive it" (Mal. 3:10). This special measure or proportion is the tithe. When worship is general, continual, and always, all we are and all we have should be offered to him. "For none of us liveth to himself, and no man dieth to himself. For whether we live, we live unto the Lord; and whether we die, we die unto the Lord: whether we live therefore, or die, we are the Lord's" (Rom. 14:7,8). If a Christian is unwilling to give the tithe to the Lord in his house and through his church, he probably is having trouble giving all of life to him in everyday living and worship.

The name that used to be applied to the burnt offering of the Old Testament meant "that which ascends." One idea was that whatever went up never came back. When one presents himself to God in worship, he must not try to take himself back. Every true believer in Christ is a Christian presenter.

What does a Christian presenter present? The answer is in the text: "I beseech you . . . that you present your bodies" (12:1). When Paul gave this admonition, the Greek language was universal, and Greek philosophy was a powerful influence throughout ussoneTHE CHRISTIAN PRESENTER 91

the world. It is, therefore, important for us to consider what the Greeks thought about the body.

There are two major viewpoints which are relevant to this discussion. On the one hand, the body was memorialized, idolized, and glorified in sculpture. The finest features of the human body, as they related to physical beauty or athletic prowess, could be seen in stone on every side. On the other hand, the body in general was considered to be evil because it was of matter, and matter was always evil. The body was considered the prison house of the soul. Greek philosophy knew nothing of the immortality of the total man but only of the immortality of the soul.

The Christian view of the body stood in bold contrast to Greek philosophy. The incarnation demonstrated the importance of the body. John surely was thinking of the body of Christ when he said, "We beheld his glory, the glory as of the only begotten of the Father, full of grace and truth" (John 1:14). The writer of Hebrews expressed this truth:

God, who at sundry times and in divers manners spake in time past unto the fathers by the prophets, hath in these last days spoken unto us by his Son, whom he hath appointed heir of all things, by whom also he made the worlds; who being the brightness of his glory, and the express image of his person, and upholding all things by the word of his power, when he had by himself purged our sins, sat down on the right hand of the Majesty on high (Heb. 1:1-3).

God is glorified in the visible. "The heavens declare the glory of God and the firmament showeth his handywork" (Ps. 19:1). "The whole earth is full of his glory" (Isa. 6:3). William Cullen Bryant said, "To him who in the love of nature holds communion with her visible forms, she speaks a various language." Browning accented the same thought: "In youth I looked into these very skies and probing their immensities I found God there, his visible power."

The high and holy God was in the body of Jesus. The resurrection of Jesus also attested to the significance of the body, which in his case did not see corruption.

In creation the first part of man to be made was the body. It should also be noted that the body is the last to be redeemed. God breathed into man's nostrils the breath of life and he became a living soul. When Paul referred to the body in Romans 12:1, as elsewhere in his writings, the total person was brought into view. Who can think wisely of the body apart from the spirit and soul of man? The presentation of the body to the Lord then means the presentation of the total person. In another place Paul exhorted:

"What? know ye not that your body is the temple of the Holy Ghost which is in you, which ye have of God, and ye are not your own? For ye are bought with a price: therefore glorify God in your body, and in your spirit, which are God's" (1 Cor. 6:19,20).

Jesus Christ was God in the flesh (1 Tim. 3:16) and he suffered "that he might reconcile both [Jew and Gentile] unto God in one body by the cross, having slain the enmity thereby" (Eph. 2:16). If the body of Jesus on the cross is essential to our salvation, then we should conclude that what happens in our bodies is essential to our acceptable service unto God.

The body of the Christian is crucial. What happens in the body affects the Spirit and the soul. The body is a point of vulnerability and an area of conflict. A problem in the body often is prior to a problem in the spirit and the soul.

Christian stewardship cannot be understood or practiced until we see the importance of presenting the body to God in worship and service, which is another way of saying the offering of the total person to God. Giving one-tenth of one's income and one-seventh of one's time falls far short of the goal of Christian stewardship. The tithe is not an end to the Christian but an important symbol of a larger and greater gift of all of life which is the Lord's. We belong to the Lord totally and what we have is his also, and we are responsible for using all to his glory.

How does the Christian present? He presents his body as a living sacrifice. Strange things have been done to the body to keep it under control and out of trouble. Simeon Stylites, a Syrian saint, is said to have kept himself alive for thirty years on top of a column and when he was too weak to stand any longer upright he had a post erected on it to which he was fastened by chains. Others have gone to extremes to make themselves uncomfortable in what they mistakenly thought was service to God.

In the Middle Ages there were people called Flagellants. They scourged themselves. In a church dimly lit by a few candles, whips of knotted cord would be distributed among the congregation. Then the candles were extinguished and the people in the dark would whip themselves to the point of bruises and lacerations.

This self-inflicted suffering is far from a living sacrifice to God. We should not make ourselves suffer for the sake of suffering. We should be willing always to suffer for Jesus' sake that his life might be seen in us.

In the Old Testament the worshiper presented a dead sacrifice to God. This typical sacrifice pointed to the death of Jesus Christ on the cross. He offered himself to God, bearing our sins in his own body on a tree, the just one suffering for the unjust. "The wages of sin is death" (Rom. 6:23). Through his death we have eternal life, and we who live in the resurrected Christ can offer a living sacrifice unto God. Paul said: "For we which live are alway delivered unto death for Jesus' sake, that the life also of Jesus might be made manifest in our mortal flesh" (2 Cor. 4:11).

The Christian life when properly perceived is a sacrifice from beginning to end or an offering to God. In the letter to the Philippians this point was emphasized. Paul affirmed: "Being confident of this very thing, that he which hath begun a good work in you will perform it until the day of Jesus Christ" (Phil. 1:6). There are two words in the verse which apply specifically and directly to sacrifice. The word "begun" refers to the beginning of the sacrifice and the word "perform" points to the conclusion of the sacrifice. The same thought may be found in Galatians 3:3: "Are ye so foolish? having begun in the Spirit, are ye now made perfect by the flesh?" The same words "begun" and "perfect" speak of the beginning and the end of the sacrifice. We do well, therefore, to understand the Christian life as a sacrifice from the beginning to the end, from the new birth to the time when God calls the Christian to his eternal home.

A Christian should not wait until he is old or until he is sick to present his body as a living sacrifice to God. When Christians of any age offer their healthy and vigorous bodies to the Lord, they surely are well pleasing in his sight. They do that which is "holy and acceptable" to him.

Jesus said, "If any man will come after me, let him deny himself, and take up his cross daily, and follow me. For whosoever will save his life shall lose it: but whosoever will lose his life for my sake, the same shall save it" (Luke 9:23-24). We bear his cross and live his cross when we present all in worship and dedicate all in service.

Paul admonished the Philippians: "Let this mind be in you, which was also in Christ Jesus" (Phil. 2:5). The mind of Christ was his willingness to leave heaven and glory and riches which he had with the Father before the world was, and come to this earth—to shame and poverty, to sin and suffering, to sacrifice and death, to the lowest and the least, to the lonely and the lost—that he might save us. "For ye know the grace of our Lord Jesus Christ, that, though he was rich, yet for your sakes he became poor, that ye through his poverty might be rich" (2 Cor. 8:9).

Epaphroditus had the mind of Christ. He went to Paul to represent the Philippian church and to stand by him and assist him in preaching the gospel. The Philippian Christians helped Paul through Epaphroditus. He served sacrificially and in total dedication. Paul wrote of him: "Because for the work of Christ he was nigh unto death, not regarding his life, to supply your lack of service toward me" (Phil. 2:30).

In times like these sacrifice and total dedication are required of us if the world is to hear the gospel and have an opportunity to trust in the Lord Jesus Christ. Bold Mission Thrust means exactly that. It is necessary for some of us to change our life-styles and deny ourselves in order for people everywhere to know our Savior whom to know aright is life eternal.

Why does the Christian present? By the mercies of God, he presents his body a living sacrifice. In the first eleven chapters of Romans, Paul expounded the great doctrine of grace. He dealt honestly with sin and declared that "all have sinned, and come short of the glory of God" (Rom. 3:23), that there is no difference between the Jew and the Gentile, that "all are under sin"; and that "every mouth may be stopped, and all the world may become guilty before God" (Rom. 3:9,19). He explained that "the wages of sin is death, but" he proclaimed that "the gift of God is eternal life through Jesus Christ our Lord" (Rom. 6:23).

According to the message in Romans, sin abounds unto death but grace superabounds unto eternal life through our wonderful Savior. The sinner has no righteousness which will commend him unto God but the righteousness of God in Jesus Christ is offered as basis for the reign of grace unto eternal life. Grace is greater than all of our sins and sufficient for all of our needs. This grace operates to give new life when the sinner believes in the Lord Jesus Christ and trusts in the righteousness of God in Jesus Christ. The glorious work of grace is expressed in such terms as justification, regeneration, sanctification, and glorification.

The unrighteous person is declared righteous by faith in the Lord Jesus Christ. The sinner who is dead in trespasses and sin is made alive by faith in the Lord Jesus Christ. The Christian grows in grace and realizes the potential of the new life in Christ as he relies upon the sanctification of the Holy Spirit. Victory over the world, the flesh, and the devil is in the power of the Holy Spirit. We are more than conquerors through him that loved us and dwells in our hearts by faith and is really present in us in the person of the Holy Spirit. In Christ, as expressed in Romans 8, there is no condemnation and there is no separation. Between these there is no defeat. The great realities of grace are the basis and background for the presentation of our bodies to God as a living sacrifice.

Every affirmation of the doctrine of grace is followed by a practical application in daily living and service. Paul closed his magnificent exposition of the resurrection with a strong admonition and appeal:

Therefore, my beloved brethren, be ye stedfast, unmoveable, always abounding in the work of the Lord, forasmuch as ye know that your labour is not in vain in the Lord. Now concerning the collection for the saints, as I have given order to the churches of Galatia, even so do ye. Upon the first day of the week let every one of you lay by him in store, as God hath prospered him, that there be no gatherings when I come (1 Cor. 15:58 to 16:2).

The same pattern is evident in his letter to Titus:

For the grace of God that bringeth salvation hath appeared to all men, Teaching us that, denying ungodliness and worldly lusts, we should live soberly, righteously, and godly, in this present world; Looking for that blessed hope, and the glorious appearing of the great God and our Saviour Jesus Christ; Who gave himself for us, that he might redeem us from all iniquity, and purify unto himself a peculiar people, zealous of good works. These things speak, and exhort, and rebuke with all authority. Let no man despise thee (Titus 2:11-15).

This is a faithful saying, and these things I will that thou affirm constantly, that they which have believed in God might be careful to maintain good works. These things are good and profitable unto men (Titus 3:8).

When there is a resentment to an appeal for Christian duty, it will disappear when the reasons for this appeal are set forth. It is important for us to see the relationship between character and conduct, believing and behaving, motivation and morals, dynamics and deeds. As Christians what we ought to do is what we want to do and what we want to do can be done through Christ who strengthens us.

Whereunto does the Christian present? The goal of a Christian is "reasonable service" which is holy and acceptable to God. The word used for service does not mean service of a deacon or a bond servant. In the New Testament it never means human service or service of man to man. It is always used of service to God. This service is not slavish or driven, but voluntary. It carries the idea of total dedication.

This word for service is closely related to the worship of God. This worship goes beyond the confines of a cathedral or a church building. What we say, do, and experience in corporate worship is true and valid only if it can be carried out into the streets and stores, factories and fields, and incorporated into everyday living. Assembling ourselves together in churches to worship God is scriptural and very important. We neglect this divinely ordained service to our peril. But presenting ourselves to God in worship wherever we are every day is the major thrust of Paul's exhortation. He called for Bold Mission Thrust.

Paul said this service is "reasonable." The word for "reasonable" is based on *logos,* the term John used of the Christ. "In the beginning was the word" (*logos,* Christ). It means wisdom, intelligence, reason, logic. The best logic is in Christ. It makes sense to worship and serve the Lord Christ. Sin and self-service, however attractive and logical they may seem early, in the end are frightfully illogical. "The wages of sin is death."

At the end of this text let us return to its beginning. Paul said, "I beseech you." The word for beseech is *paraclete.* Paraclete is the Holy Spirit, the Comforter, the Teacher, the Friend. In the love, compassion, persuasion, and power of the Holy Spirit, "I beseech you" to present yourselves to God in worship and service.

One of the most moving experiences of my life came to me in Ogbomosho, Nigeria. Baptist work there may be the strongest and best we have in foreign missions. There are large Baptist churches, a great hospital, an outstanding seminary, and other Christian ministries. I was impressed by all of these evidences of God's blessings.

On the last day of our visit we went to a nearby cemetery. Graves of Southern Baptist missionaries were there. I noticed markers which told when the missionaries came to Nigeria and when they died. Some died after only one year of service. More than one hundred years ago the way was rough. Malaria and other diseases made it difficult for them to survive. As the first missionaries died, others took their places. They must have been convinced that the gospel must be given to Nigeria even if it meant they must die.

God blessed their living sacrifice and the fruits of their labors are evident everywhere in that land. I was more than impressed. I was inspired.

Today, now, here, all of us—the call is to give and live, sacrifice and serve in Bold Mission Thrust that the people may know God through our Lord Jesus Christ.

William Henry Crouch has served as pastor of Providence Baptist Church, Charlotte, North Carolina, since 1969. He is a native of Asheville, North Carolina, and a graduate of Southern Baptist Theological Seminary.

11
ADVENTURES IN FAITH

Isaiah 54:1-10

Marse Grant reported recently in the *Biblical Recorder:* "There's a new excitement in Southern Baptist life these days. This is our strongest single impression after attending the recent Southern Baptist Executive Committee in Nashville." As a member of the Foreign Mission Board, I can echo this sentiment.

Why are Southern Baptists excited? What has initiated a renewed adventure in faith that has challenged Southern Baptists together to attempt great things for God? The excitement of attempting great things has generated a feeling among Southern Baptists which cannot be described by business as usual.

Missions has been the heartbeat of our denomination, and the decision to move ahead with a Bold Mission Thrust has provided us with a real challenge. The commitment of Southern Baptists "to enable every person in the world to have the opportunity to hear and respond to the gospel by the year 2000" is indeed BOLD. But God is opening doors of opportunity! Our seminaries are full of eager, dedicated, and talented young people preparing themselves to go into the field to reap the harvest.

The key to our mission program is the local church and individual Christian commitment. It will require a well-balanced effort on the home front if we are to reach the goal of sharing the gospel with the world by 2000. Can this Bold Mission Thrust bring excitement to our own church? How can we find our place in such an adventure in faith? What part should my church—our church— play in making possible such a Bold Mission Thrust?

Isaiah spoke to Israel in captivity and had as his theme the coming of the King in his glory. Chapter 53 is the prediction of the Suffering Messiah: one who would give himself for the sins of the world. Chapter 54 inaugurates a new covenant with God's people. They were to sing and break forth with singing because conditions could be changed for them. The Lord was going to use them for his divine purposes of saving the world. Isaiah predicted they would emerge from the epics of persecution and slavery stronger in spirit and in numbers. The Lord had chosen them and wed them as a bride. They would no longer be barren! In magnificent language he described the splendor of the new age about to dawn as they emerged from the darkness of despair brought about by their exile to the dazzling light of a new day.

Notice God's challenge to Israel as found in verse 2: "Enlarge the place of your tent, and let the curtains of your habitations be stretched out; hold not back, lengthen your cords and strengthen your stakes" (RSV). Remember the ancient Israelite was a nomad who lived primarily in tents. Such language was very descriptive and easily understood.

The tent was made of canvas supported by poles. The tallest pole was in the center and the others suspended the curtains or flaps that covered the sides of the tent. Pegs were driven into the ground to hold down the sides of the tent and to hold the poles upright. It was essential that the pegs be driven deep to keep the tent secure from the wind and the storms of the desert.

Build Up

"Enlarge the place of your tent, and let the curtains of your habitations be stretched out." Israel was told that the days of barrenness were over and that God would be increasing their number. As a family increased, the ancient nomad enlarged his tent by opening out the flaps or stretching out the curtain. Isaiah's prophecy was the revival of confidence and hope. His message from God was heard as some forty-two thousand persons were released from the Babylonian captivity. By the time of Jesus, some three million inhabitants were living in Israel.

The home front is important. The local church is the very center of our strength as Southern Baptists. We must provide the message, the messengers, and the means for the Bold Mission Thrust. Israel was to build a permanent habitation that would be large enough to accommodate all the children who would come.

One of the basic principles of growth is to prepare for it. The essential ingredients are vision and faith. Herein lies the great difference among churches: Some churches have vision while others seem unable to catch a vision and to build with faith. "Where there is no vision, the people perish" (Prov. 29:18). We must believe that God is going to do great things for us in our communities and prepare ourselves for the growth that will come as we faithfully witness.

Providence Baptist Church is a product of vision, faith, and wise planning. Twenty-six years ago men and women of faith decided to launch out and deliberately expand by starting a new church in southeast Charlotte. Mostly open fields and countryside surrounded the site selected by the Mecklenburg Baptist Association for the beginning of the new mission. Churches in the association contributed money, members, and their ministers who preached for the new congregation on Sunday afternoons until a full-time pastor was secured.

Since that time people have come from all over the world and settled in southeast Charlotte. A multitude of people live in the houses and apartments which now make up the community which our growing church serves. A shopping center is only a few blocks away, and perhaps thousands of persons ride daily over the boulevard that passes by the front of the present twenty-five-acre church property. In a short span of twenty-six years of organized life the church is among the leading churches of the North Carolina Baptist Convention in size, gifts, and ministries. From eighty-eight charter members our church has grown to over twenty-one hundred members. This is an exciting story of an adventure in faith: God's people responding to a call to "build up!" It requires unselfish effort on the part of churches in an association to implement a vision of need for the future with faith and diligent planning.

Dig In

"Hold not back"—"Spare not"—Israel was told that to enlarge her tents she had to have long ropes that were strong and had to drive tent pegs deep into the soil. This was necessary to hold the tents upright. Israel was told not to spare anything needed to gain strength so that the tent would stand firm, stable, and permanent. If Bold Mission Thrust is to be accomplished around the world, we must keep our churches strong and alive.

The prophet Isaiah was dealing with *attitude!* We are on God's mission and seeking to be God's people. If God opens the door for advance, we must be willing to walk through the door of challenge. Every city in America is growing and the population expansion is unbelievable. We must catch the vision of the needs of America and of her cities and what Christ can do for them. If we are to win the world, our attitudes on the home front must be those of expectancy and willingness to prepare for growth.

The prophet was dealing with *ability!* God always gives the resources for the task. He has promised that. He never expects more of us than he has provided. He gives talent and wealth to our people and to our churches for the accomplishment of his mission. We must remember that to whom much is given—much is expected!

The prophet is dealing also with *action!* Our faith must come alive! James has reminded us that "faith without works is dead." God calls for responses that require effort, foresight, and outlay of resources. It comes down to our willingness to trust God, to be submissive, and to respond according to what God has entrusted to us. That is the reason that stewardship and life-style are so important to us as Southern Baptists. If the Bold Mission Thrust is to be successful, we must not hold back our resources.

Local missions is a difficult task in a day when churches are jealous of their numbers and seek only their own growth. Our fear of new fellowships is contrary to the heart of missions. Strong churches should be willing to share wealth and members with new communities so that new congregations can grow into strong churches.

Providence Baptist Church is today the second largest contributor to the Cooperative Program in our association. We, through our gifts, add to the impact for Christ in the community, reaching many more persons than otherwise could have been expected.

We need to capture the excitement of expanding—stretching out—digging in. We need to direct our attitudes, abilities, and actions to our own locality with grave concern for winning it to Christ. The "30,000 movement" may be over but the need is still with us as America grows each year.

Move Out

"Move out"—"For you will spread abroad to the right and to the left, and your descendants will possess the nations and will people the desolate cities" (54:3, RSV). Judah had been reduced to a tiny territory and the prophet predicted a peaceful expansion beyond her borders. She would embrace and share with nearby people her spiritual treasures.

God has many children! He is not just our Father! His interest and love go to all mankind. It is sometimes hard to imagine the universality of God's love. God has a purpose for mankind! Jesus died for all men. Redemption is to be universal. We have many evidences to show that all types of persons respond to God's message. The church that obediently and boldly declares God's message of love and redemption can expect results.

God calls us to carry the message! We are his instruments and the messengers who must move out. God enters into fellowship with his chosen people for the redemption of the entire human race.

We recognize Africa, Japan, South America, and other fields as ready for spiritual harvest. But so are most cities in our country. The large, fast influx of persons to our cities is staggering! Houses are not being built fast enough to house the people finding our churches. New communities are growing up around us. Shall we turn a deaf ear to their needs and send all our resources to other parts of the world? Our vision is of home *and* faraway places.

We decided to become involved with local missions because we remembered that we were given life by deliberate expansion of the associational missions program. Through faith, with excitement, we have in these twenty-six years helped sponsor three new congregations in Charlotte:

Carmel Baptist Church is now a thriving congregation. In 1965, one hundred of our own members with a gift of twenty-eight thousand dollars from our building fund began to stand alone as a church. It is today one of the leading churches in our convention.

Sharon Baptist Church was an outgrowth of our associational missions program also. In 1971 our church joined forces to co-sponsor our second mission church. We called the late Dr. C. C. Warren (former pastor of First Baptist Church of Charlotte and former president of the Southern Baptist Convention—and leader in the "30,000 movement") to head the new mission venture. We built their first structure and have been thrilled to see them become another strong Southern Baptist church in our community.

This past year our church has joined forces with the association, Sharon Baptist, Carmel Baptist, and Matthews Baptist in cosponsoring the Candlewyck Baptist Mission located six miles south of our church. This mission has available thirteen and a half acres of beautiful land provided by the Association and a budget of twenty-five thousand dollars this year. My own excitement over the mission has been heightened by the calling of my father, Dr. W. Perry Crouch (former executive secretary of North Carolina Baptist Convention) as mission pastor to help it grow into a church. The mission already has twenty-two members who are meeting in the Charlotte Latin School on Providence Road. It is obvious that the investment of time, money, and people have paid its dividends manyfold. As a mission of strong mission-minded people we have developed a large tent from which to minister. Recognizing our debt to others, who made it possible for us to have life, we gladly reach out to join hands with our association to help give life to other new churches in our community. This we wish continually to do. We wish never to be a dying church as depicted by one artist.

Commissioned to paint the picture of a dying church, this artist went to the task with great enthusiasm. Finally, the day came when the painting was to be unveiled. Everyone present expected to see a run-down church, badly in need of painting, worn-out carpets, and splintered pews. Instead they saw a very neat, elegant church, well appointed with plush carpeting and bright shining light fixtures. At first they were deeply puzzled over the artist's interpretation. Then someone called attention to a small box in the corner. It was covered with cobwebs and dust, obviously very rarely used. Still legible were the letters: *M-i-s-s-i-o-n-s*. What an indictment! To build a large tent and not stretch out to others.

We are attempting to do what God challenged Israel to do. We have "built up" our tent on the home front. We have put our pegs down deep and not spared even our own people. We are reaching out to people in Charlotte as well as to others all over the world to share with them the good news of redemption. That is an exciting adventure in faith!

William J. Cumbie has served as the executive director of the Mount Vernon Baptist Association, Alexandria, Virginia since November 1, 1957. He is a native of Macon, Georgia, and is a graduate of Eastern Baptist Theological Seminary.

12

A NEW TOMORROW

Joshua 3:5

"To have a reason to get up in the morning, it is necessary to possess a guiding principle. A belief of some kind. A bumper sticker, if you will. People in cars on busy freeways call to each other: BOYCOTT GRAPES; comfort each other: HONK IF YOU LOVE JESUS; antagonize with statements of faith: I HAVE A DREAM, TOO—LAW AND ORDER. Ordinary people feel joy, love, fear and sometimes—and this can be devastating—an agonizing sense of guilt and loss."[1]

Southern Baptists are now involved in Bold Mission Thrust
  —Bold Going
  —Bold Growing
  —Bold Giving
  —and Bold Advance

We are in a here-and-now hour girding up for our ministry to serve this day and generation and in some measure to fulfill the charge given by Jesus "Go therefore and make disciples of all nations" (Matt. 28:19, RSV). It is well to remember a great statement attributed to Thomas Jefferson: "I like the dreams of the future better than the history of the past." That's what Bold Mission Thrust is all about—translating the dreams of God's people into reality.

The Bible background for this message is in the crossing narratives of the book of Joshua. The people of God-called Israel had wandered for forty years and had been assured of God's guidance by signs. They had a pillar of fire by night and a pillar of cloud by day. Moses and all of those with him who had failed to live up to God's clear command to love and to obey him with all their heart and mind and strength had died. Now a new leader appeared. "And Joshua the son of Nun was full of the spirit of wisdom, for Moses had laid his hands upon him" (Deut. 34:9, RSV). Joshua was a God-appointed leader and his leadership had been authenticated by the people.

They were preparing to go into the Promised Land. Two spies surveyed Jericho and were saved by Rahab, the harlot. They reported and the people were ready to move in and take the land. Joshua stopped them and called on them to be spiritually prepared: "Sanctify yourselves; for tomorrow the Lord will do wonders among you" (Josh. 3:5, RSV).

A new tomorrow awaits those who are ready to meet God's requirement: "Sanctify yourselves!" The ancient people responded to God's call, and God did wonders in their midst. "Every Christian . . . is sanctified in the sense that he is dedicated or consecrated to God by the power of the Spirit and by his own act of faith. . . . One dedicates himself to God and separates himself from all that opposes his consecration to God."[2] The need of our time is the rediscovery of the extraordinary simplicity and power of total surrender to the will of God. C. S. Lewis' experience recorded in his autobiography is instructive. He tells of his conversion from atheism to theism and from theism to Christianity. He changed from believing there is no God to believing that there is a God to believing that Jesus Christ is Savior and God. On the night he surrendered his life and gave in to God, he was most dejected and reluctant. He pictured himself as a prodigal brought in kicking, struggling, resentful, and darting his eyes in every direction for a chance to escape. Lewis discovered "the hardness of God is kinder than the softness of men, and His compulsion is our liberation."[3] God's invitation to you is not the hardness of a demand for perfection, but the softness of a merciful God who "so loved the world that he gave his only begotten Son, that whosoever believes in him should not perish but have eternal life" (John 3:16, RSV).

A new tomorrow awaits those who are willing to risk for ministry and witness in the name of the Lord Jesus. Albert Camus tells a parable "about two strangers walking together one night on the streets of Amsterdam. One of them terminates the conversation at a bridge: 'I'll leave you near this bridge. I never cross a bridge at night. It's the result of a vow. Suppose, after all, that someone should jump into the water. One of two things—either you do likewise to fish him out and, in cold weather, you run a great risk! Or you forsake him there and suppressed drives sometimes leave one strangely aching. Goodnight.'"[4]

Many contemporary Christians are suppressing the Spirit-given drives. They fear being involved in the work of the Lord. They fear being judged by God. And they are rendered impotent by their fear. Whenever God's people miss a new tomorrow, they are left strangely aching.

What are some of the risks which Southern Baptists as people of God need to take for a new tomorrow? We need to risk the whole gospel. Years ago, one church adopted the slogan "the whole gospel for the whole world." Others speak eloquently to the necessity of biblical and theological integrity in the message we offer to the world. If we want to address the whole world, we must take the risk of seeing the world as it really is.

Anytime one searches for statistics about the number of Christians in the world, he comes face to face with the enormous difficulty of finding reliable information. Since the available statistics are not gathered on the same basis with the same understanding of religious commitment and, since ethnic considerations and nationalism get mixed into the data, one must be careful how he uses the information. Franklin H. Littell compiled a table for the 1979 Britannica Book of the Year. He gave 968,184,100 for the total Christian population in the world. Even if this most optimistic estimate is accepted, less than one of every four persons in the world can be assumed to be Christian. Less than 60 percent of the world's population is reported as having a religious commitment of any kind. By New Testament standards, "every one who believes that Jesus is the Christ is a child of God" (1 John 5:1, RSV). The awesome and overwhelming responsibility for sharing the gospel with more than three fourths of the world's people who are without Christ and without hope in the world requires us to take the risk of the whole gospel for the whole world.

We must take the risk of a renewed church. *Revival* is very much a part of Southern Baptists' vocabulary and program. The spiritual renewal discovered in protracted preaching meetings of earlier days is desperately needed in contemporary urban America. Business as usual and a play-it-safe mentality block the renewal of the Spirit and render the people of God impotent and strangely aching.

In the midst of a deep division in a congregation over how to seek renewal, a dialogue developed between two deacons. One was a classic representative of the best of the deep-South Baptist life. The other was a black Baptist who had escaped the bondage of color. As these deacons talked and prayed about their church, they learned that their Christian experiences had begun in a remarkably similar way. Each had accepted Christ at a revival meeting. They discovered, as one said, "That's where we all started"; not so much in a revival meeting as in a personal life-changing experience with the Lord.

Bold Mission Thrust awaits the rediscovery of the simplicity and sublimity of how we began. A vital, ongoing personal experience with the Lord is the sure way to church renewal and revival. And such an experience is essential for those who want to be a part of God's new tomorrow.

A new tomorrow awaits those who are willing to risk a radical commitment to the Lord Jesus Christ.

Baptists are properly proud of their history, a history filled with heroes. Among these is James Ireland, an early Virginia Baptist pastor. Born in Scotland in 1748, Ireland settled in Shenandoah County, Virginia, as a schoolteacher. Reared as a Presbyterian, Ireland shared the popular scorn for the Baptists and had made a solemn oath never to unite with them. Nicholas Fain, a member of Smith's Creek Baptist Church in Shenandoah, was the instrument of the Holy Spirit to awaken James Ireland's deep religious nature. Described as ones "who possessed what he professed," Fain and Ireland became the nucleus of a group concerned with the spiritual state of their lives.

John Pickett, a traveling dancing master turned evangelist by the preaching of the Separate Baptists in North Carolina, returned to Fauquier, Virginia, a changed man. He witnessed to his neighbors. At the invitation of the Shenandoah group, he came sixty miles and preached to them for two days about personal, vital, and experimental religion. Ireland was stirred so deeply that he rushed 100 miles to secure a proper baptism and to satisfy his mind and heart about the principles of the Baptists. He spent several weeks in the company of John Garrard and Jeremiah Walker, evangelists commissioned by the Ketoctin Association. Finally convinced, he accepted the insistent invitation of Garrard and Walker to share in the preaching at meetings conducted on their way to Sandy Creek. After preaching in several meetings, Ireland was baptized by Samuel Harris and ordained as an itinerant evangelist.

In November, 1769, Ireland went into Culpeper and spent the night at Captain Thomas McClanahan's. There he was served notice that if he met his appointment to preach the next day, he would be arrested. He wrote about his anquish of soul in making a decision: "I sat down and counted the cost. Freedom or prison? It admitted of no dispute. Having ventured all upon Christ, I determined to suffer all for him."

And suffer he did. He preached the next day, was arrested and spent the winter in wretched quarters of a colonial jail. Although only twenty-one, this man of God suffered permanent health damage for the sake of the gospel.[5] Where are the twentieth-century versions of such high commitment? Who will follow in Ireland's steps?

Another risk we must take, if we are to share God's new tomorrow, is the risk of sacrificial giving.

There is a church I've known well for over twenty-five years. In the late forties, the church sent 25 percent of its gifts to missions through the Cooperative Program, saved 25 percent toward a much needed new building, and spent 50 percent on its local program. Over the years, the pattern has slipped to only 15 percent for all missions (Cooperative Program, Associational Missions, and designated special offerings). The building continues to cost 25 percent and the rest is spent on staff and local program.

This trend is widespread among us. Our effective buying-power giving falls further and further behind the vision of a world in need.

Because of my assignment, I hear others preach regularly. I preach regularly too. Neither I nor the preachers I hear preach very much about sacrifice. Oh, I don't mean the kind of distortion that says you've got to hurt in order to be spiritual. I don't believe that; I don't believe the Bible teaches that. But the Bible does teach us to set priorities. Margaret Slocum, a Sunday School teacher at the First Baptist Church of Macon, Georgia, led me to decide to follow Jesus and accept him as Savior and Lord. She gave me my first Bible. On the flyleaf, she wrote, "Seek ye first the kingdom of God, and his righteousness; and all these things shall be added unto you. Matt. 6:33" That kind of priority setting will make a difference in the world. It will make a difference for persons, for churches, and for the denomination.

We live in an affluent society. There is every indication of the highest standard of living in our history. Despite the ravages of inflation, God's people have a lot of God's money in their pockets. I believe that we who preach are under a divine mandate to claim those dollars for the Lord and his priority of evangelizing and congregationalizing the whole world.

On a personal level, have you and I examined our own life-styles and spending patterns in the light of Christ's clear call to self-denial (Matt. 16:24)? Have we looked at our church budgets and their allocations to world missions through the eyes of the Great Commission? Do our Cooperative Program allocations—state and SBC—accurately reflect the priorities of winning the lost and nurturing the saved?

We may manipulate the percentages and change the divisions, but we can never come close to adequately funding the missions programs until the people of God catch again the vision of a lost world and do something about sharing their riches in order to win that world to Christ.

Lest we think that the lost people are somewhere in the Third World, we need to remember that secularism and indifference has made America a mission field.

I often watch the streams of traffic leaving the nation's capital carrying thousands to their suburban homes. Every survey we've made over the years indicates that only one or two has a connection with a church in the area. Typical is a young man who came to me on Good Friday and asked, "What's this Easter stuff all about?" Later, he came again and asked me, in straightforward terms, to help him understand how to become a Christian. He refused to make the commitment and to receive Jesus as Savior and Lord. We are still talking about his decision. There are untold thousands like him all across America.[6]

The Lord of the harvest calls us to see again the "fields already white to harvest" (John 4:35). At home and overseas, millions await the response of the people who, like James Ireland's friend, Nicholas Fain, "possess what they profess."

Bold Mission Thrust breaks open the possibility of doing something great for God in our time. What are we waiting for? Has the call of God captured our hearts and minds so that we have a missionary vision to "enter the promised land"?

There are no clouds now, no pillars of fire to guide us. But there is the assurance of God's power in vital churches and in the lives of persons who have experienced that power again and again. We believe that God does make a difference in our lives, and he enables believers to reach out in caring concern for persons of all situations.

God has a way! First Corinthians 1:26-31 describes us well: "Now remember what you were, my brothers, when God called you. From the human point of view few of you were wise or powerful or of high social standing. God purposely chose what the world considers nonsense in order to shame the wise, and he chose what the world considers nonsense in order to shame the powerful. He chose what the world looks down on and despises and thinks is nothing, in order to destroy what the world thinks is important. This means that no one can boast in God's presence. But God has brought you into union with Christ Jesus, and God has made Christ to be our wisdom. By him we are put right with God; we become God's holy people and are set free. So then, as the scripture says, 'Whoever wants to boast must boast of what the Lord has done' " (TEV).

That's a vision of a new tomorrow for the people of God who respond to God's call: "Sanctify yourselves; for tomorrow the Lord will do wonders among you" (Josh. 3:5, RSV).

So pack your bags; get ready to move out. Let's go for God and use our hour of opportunity so that God indeed may bring a new tomorrow to a lost and broken world, for his glory and the blessing of all mankind!

Notes

[1]Guest, Judith, *Ordinary People,* Reader's Digest Condensed Books, Volume 5, 1976, p. 331.

[2]Conner, W. T., *The Gospel of Redemption* (Nashville: Broadman Press, 1945), p. 194.

[3]Lewis, C.S., *Surprised By Joy* (New York: Harcourt, Brace and Co., 1956), p. 228-229.

[4]Camus, Albert, *The Fall* (New York: Alfred Knopf, 1959). p. 15.

[5]Ryland, Garnett, *The Baptists of Virginia 1699-1926* (Richmond: The Virginia Baptist Board of Mission and Education, 1955), pp. 47 ff., 63 ff.

Moore, John S. and Lumpkin, William L., *Meaningful Moments in Virginia Baptist Life 1715-1972* (Sesquicentennial Celebration of Baptist General Association of Virginia, 1973), p. 13.

   [6]"The Unchurched: Believers at Heart?", *Christianity Today,* July 21, 1978, p. 52.

Keener Pharr has been the director of the
education division of the Florida Baptist Convention since 1969. He is a native of Gadsden,
Alabama, and a graduate of Southwestern Baptist Theological Seminary.

13
BOLD CHURCH STRATEGY

1 Chronicles 29:5; 2 Timothy 2:15; Colossians 3:23

The Pine Terrace Baptist Church in Milton, Florida, moved
during 1979 to implement the Bold Mission Thrust commitments
of our Convention. The pastor, the Reverend Joe Floyd, says, "If
every church will dream big and put prayers, planning, leadership,
and work into implementing their dreams . . . God will bless their
efforts!"

This church adopted the motto "Dream Big" as a church
slogan. Already they are experiencing record attendance in Sunday

School and Church Training. This is the third year in which they have recorded significant results in baptisms, additions by letter, and stewardship responses.

Last summer, the pastor shared his dreams with the deacons and church council members, challenging them to start planning for a Bold Mission Thrust. The church council spent six hours "dreaming big" and planning for a Bold Mission Thrust. They sought God's will as to what he would have their church members be and do in reaching the world for Christ by the year 2000. The church is reaching out to win persons to Christ, increased giving to missions, and provided new facilities. They are challenging more members to become soul-winners as a basic requirement in Bold Mission Thrust.

The key to this testimony is that good planning and preparation always precedes achievement. It should also be noted that the beginning of good planning is leadership. The pastor, other church staff, and key church leaders must deliberately face this requirement and provide high quality leadership.

If we experience a Bold Mission Thrust in our denomination, it will happen when key church leaders roll up their sleeves and get with the task of planning the Bold Growing, Bold Going, and Bold Giving activities needed in every church.

Let us identify four basic requirements of leadership in developing a bold church strategy.

Let's Get Right!—1 Chronicles 29:5

David was committed to building a Temple . . . a house of worship . . . a symbol of God's presence and leadership in the midst of the people. In the opening words of this chapter, he challenged the people to contribute all that was needed to build a beautiful Temple. David told them of the specific preparation being made for building the Temple for the Lord God.

Then he came to the bottom line—the basic need for leadership commitment and involvement. He spoke of the human resources needed to complete the project—"and who then is willing to consecrate his services this day unto the Lord" (Chron. 29:5)?

Analyze David's appeal and ask these questions—Am I usable? Am I able? Am I available?

"*Who then* . . . ." Each of us in our places of service must serve the Lord to the best of our ability. We also need to seek out others whom God has called and place before them the same challenge. "Who then?"

"*Is willing* . . . ." One of the great, contemporary needs is for workers who are willing to get involved—to get under the load and give of their best in committed leadership. One of the basic needs of Bold Mission Thrust is for willing workers.

"*To consecrate his services* . . . ." Dwight L. Moody is quoted as saying: "God is already ready to use all of us that is usable." This reminds us of the need for our lives to be as clean vessels unto honor and not dishonor!

"*This day* . . . ." These words remind us of the urgency of our Lord as he gave priority to his earthly ministry, "I must be about my Father's business" (Luke 2:49). We need to demonstrate that same urgent priority in leading Bold Mission Thrust—"while it is yet day!"

"*Unto the Lord!*" The apostle Paul also reminded his fellow workers to do their work "as unto the Lord!" The implication is clear. It is possible for church leaders to play to the grandstand, seeking the applause and approbation of men. David and the apostle Paul join in calling us to a proper motivation in our leadership "as unto the Lord!"

Let's Get Ready!—2 Timothy 2:15

It is better to look ahead and prepare than look back and despair! The difference is planning! Paul wrote to a young churchman named Timothy and urged him to get ready for his leadership role through study and preparation.

The planning process helps us look to the future with purpose. It is not a question of whether we will make good plans. Not to plan is one approach to planning itself.

Planning does not exclude the role of the Holy Spirit in guiding the affairs and destiny of a church. Church planning begins with the assumption that God has given us his Holy Spirit. He has endowed us with God-given abilities and special gifts. He has called us to a leadership role in the church. He assumes we will use these abilities and gifts in fulfilling our leadership responsibilities while *fully depending* on the leadership of the Holy Spirit.

Look again at the opening chapters of the book of Acts and see a group of bold church leaders engaging in basic planning activities. They prayed; they reviewed special needs; they nominated and elected a new worker; they recommitted themselves to a bold mission thrust; they went to work preaching, teaching, and healing; and then they enjoyed the blessings of God upon their labors.

The times in which we live challenge church leaders to think big, act big, and plan in such a way that the work of God done through our churches may truly become a Bold Mission Thrust.

The following preparation actions are basic and essential to a Bold Mission Thrust strategy in our churches and denomination.

Create and maintain a spiritual atmosphere. A church characterized by love, joy, excitement, boldness, and expectancy is ready to do great things for God. When church leaders and members surrender to the lordship of Christ and yield daily to his leadership, their lives will reflect a contagious love for one another and a constant compassion for the lost. A spiritual atmosphere makes possible the planning and implementing of growing, going, and giving activities.

Acts 2:46-47 describes this important foundational step, "And they, continuing daily with one accord in the temple, and breaking bread from house to house, did eat their meat with gladness and singleness of heart, praising God, and having favour with all the people. And the Lord added to the church daily such as should be saved."

Duke McCall, writing some time ago in *The Tie,* made an insightful observation concerning the need for spiritual expectancy in our churches when he said: "What the world needs is more people who are not conformed to this world, who are not complaining about the absence of spiritual power; who are not sitting around wishing for a return to the simple ways of the good old days . . . but, who believe that tomorrow a gracious God might conceivably use them to turn our world upside down for Jesus Christ."

That kind of concern and commitment, coupled with good planning will create and maintain a spiritual atmosphere which is essential to a Bold Mission Thrust.

Enlist and train the key leaders. The church council is responsible for Bold Mission Thrust strategy planning in the church. They should represent the finest and best leadership the church can provide. The pastor should be the catalyst and coordinator of all planning activity. He must help lay leaders discover their spiritual gifts and utilize their talents in advancing the cause of Christ and the work of a church. If lay leaders can become excited about a Bold Mission Thrust—the sky is the limit!

Through the years, Tom Landry has demonstrated great skill as a winning football coach. A news story appeared in the *Dallas Morning News* some time ago which quoted Tom Landry explaining to reporters why two key players were not used in an important football game. He said, "They were not playing up to my performance levels." Upon further questioning, the coach described three levels of performance for Dallas Cowboy football players.

—The ability to execute the plays

—A competitive spirit

—Consistency in performance

Wouldn't it be great if our church leaders qualified through study, training, and planning to have the ability needed to lead Bold Mission Thrust; to get excited about their work and to be fully consistent in performing it? We would truly experience a Bold Mission Thrust if our key leaders performed on these levels.

Plan and develop Bold Mission Thrust plans. Someone has said, "It is better to plan to succeed and fail in the deed . . . than plan to fail and always succeed!"

There are four practical steps in planning a bold church strategy:

First, dream big. What does God want your church to be and do three, five years from now? How many people do you see who should be reached by our church? How large is your vision?

This planning step makes us reflect on the kind of future we want and how our church fits into it. It will open up challenging new ideas and call us to our knees when we realize the scope of the task before us.

Second, discover needs. The First Baptist Church of Fort Walton Beach, Florida, led by their pastor, James L. Monroe, planned a series of Sunday evening discussion groups structured around a study of needs in their church. The membership was assigned to discussion groups to consider critical needs and propose responses which the church council could use in detailed planning.

Third, determine priorities and goals. This important activity follows logically the first two steps of dreaming big and discovering needs. The Bold Mission Thrust priorities of Bold Growing, Bold Going, and Bold Giving are biblical in origin and practical in contemporary application. They are at the heart of the Great Commission and follow the example of our Lord in his earthly ministry. Church leaders should consider these commitments as they identify needs and determine priorities.

Goals should be set in the context of these specific priorities. Goals should be clearly defined and challenging. As a church sets goals—ask and answer questions such as the following.

(1) How many new people should our church win and baptize by next September 30?

(2) What should our Sunday School enrollment and attendance be in order to quality as a Bold Growing church?

(3) How can we train our members in witnessing and visitation techniques?

(4) Could our church sponsor the beginning of a new Sunday School or church-type mission?

(5) How many persons could our church encourage to commit themselves to full-time missionary service?

(6) Could we encourage and support some of our members in the Mission Service Corps?

(7) Are there groups of persons prevented from church attendance by special circumstances that we should reach out to through mission ministry activities?

(8) What should our giving goals be in support of a Bold Mis-

sion Thrust in number of tithers, in Cooperative Program giving, in special missions gifts, in associational missions support?

It has been well said, "If you don't care where you are going, any road will take you there." If, on the other hand, we are committed to Bold Mission Thrust and its priorities—our goals should clarify that commitment and become guideposts along the way toward successful achievement.

God can forgive our failure to reach goals that are too ambitious, easier than he can forgive our contentment with goals that are too shallow. If our goals don't challenge our faith—they are too small!

Fourth, design activities and projects. The aim of this planning step is to find ways of implementing and achieving the goals which have been set. Too often our commitments, priorities, and goals are "preached and publicized" but not "planned and implemented!" Be sure to assign leadership responsibility for activities and allocate resources in keeping with priorities.

Developing a Bold Mission Thrust strategy will be determined by several factors: the depth of the church's commitment to biblical missions; the effort by key leaders to make Bold Mission Thrust a significant part of its local church program; the willingness of the members to make it happen; the commitment of key church leaders to subjugate personal desires and ambitions for the good of the church.

Let's Get Excited! Colossians 3:23

The apostle Paul appealed for a worthy response when he said, "Whatsoever ye do, do it heartily, as to the Lord, and not unto men."

Bold Mission Thrust in the eighties represents a great challenge for our churches and denomination. Success depends upon key leaders developing a strong sense of mission concerning its biblical commitments and contemporary challenges. Church leaders need to get excited in the best sense of the word.

The word *enthusiasm* is a combination of meaningful words, which in their root meaning says that "God is in us!" If he is, why aren't we excited and enthusiastic . . .

About the work of the Holy Spirit? Paul said, "I can do all things through Christ which strengtheneth me" (Phil. 4:13). His testimony is that God keeps on pouring strength into us, however much is required for the task at hand.

About reaching and winning people to Christ and church membership? There are few problems in our churches that would not be eliminated or alleviated by a movement of God's Spirit causing people to be saved in great numbers.

About seeing people grow and develop in the Lord? The happiest people in a church are those who are daily experiencing new truths in God's Word, appropriating these to their personal lives, and reflecting spiritual growth through Christian attitudes and action.

About God's blessings upon our work? When we set goals, make plans, work hard, and then are blessed with significant progress, there will be great rejoicing among God's people.

Let's Get Going! James 1:22

The half brother of our Lord recognized it is easier to pray for, preach about, plan, and promote programs than it is to perform the hard work required to bring plans to fruition. The time is at hand for us to "become doers of the word, and not hearers only" in leading Bold Mission Thrust.

For most of us, it is a matter of commitment. At this critical point in Bold Mission Thrust, we must face the question, How committed are we? If we let the first years of this significant denominational effort pass without doing anything about it, could we respond affirmatively to David's words, "Who then is willing to consecrate his services *this day* unto the Lord?" (1 Chron. 29:5,6).

It is said that the famous violinist, Fritz Kreisler, was walking down a back street of a European city when he heard the liquid, penetrating tones of a violin. He stopped and listened. The music came again. Eagerly, he followed the sound and found a shabby little secondhand store. He offered to buy the violin but was told it was not for sale.

"That this beautiful voice might be doomed to silence under the glass case of a collector," said Kreisler, "was a tragedy that rent my heart. From that moment I was determined to have it and to endow it with life. I laid siege to the place and gave the owner no peace. At last he took it from its resting place to grant me a small concession—the privilege to play it. I opened the case and took it out. I poured my whole soul into it. I played as a man might play for his life's ransom."

When the great musician finished, there was silence except for the halting words of the owner who stood pale and deeply moved. He said, "I have no right to it. It belongs to you. Keep it. Go out into the world and let it be heard."

So it is with our lives. When we think what God can do with them, surely we want God to have them. Our discords can be changed to beautiful melodies when our lives are placed in his hands.

Persistence and determination, growing out of a commitment to be used of God will make us the kind of church leaders these times require!

"Who then . . . ?"

Daniel G. Vestal has served as pastor of the First Baptist Church, Midland, Texas, since May 2, 1976. He is a native of Waco, Texas, and a graduate of Southwestern Baptist Theological Seminary.

14

A THEOLOGY OF COOPERATION

1 Corinthians 3:1-9

The chief clerk in a department store was trying to dislodge a crate from a storage-room door. He was working hard when an assistant clerk offered to help. For the next couple of minutes on opposite sides of the crate they both worked, lifted, puffed, and wheezed. But the crate wouldn't budge. Finally the assistant clerk said, "I don't believe we'll ever get this box out of the storage room." "Get it out?" the chief clerk responded, "I'm trying to get it in."

Cooperation is important in every realm of life. But in the enterprise of extending the kingdom of God there is no more valuable quality than unity. One reason God has blessed Southern Baptists has been their ability to cooperate in the cause of world missions. The existence of associations, state conventions, and a national convention is all based on voluntary cooperation. Without bishops, synods, or presbyteries, Southern Baptists have joined together in a spirit of mutual trust and common purpose to fulfill the Great Commission.

Perhaps there is no place where cooperation is more graphically demonstrated than in the way we as Southern Baptists finance our world mission enterprise. The program which has enabled us to pool our resources for the support of missions is what we call the Cooperative Program. The Cooperative Program, though a human program, is based on some biblical and theological principles that are important for us to understand.

It is not always easy for individuals or churches to be cooperative, and there are several reasons for it. First, we are highly individualistic. The genius of the American way has emphasized the right of the individual, and I would not for one moment minimize that constitutional privilege. But the emphasis of Scripture is not so much on individual rights as it is on individual responsibility. And one of the primary individual responsibilities mentioned in the Bible is to love our neighbors as we do ourselves. Another reason we find it difficult to be cooperative is that we are highly independent. Each of us likes to think of himself as self-sufficient, self-made, self-reliant. The popular clichés, "Do your own thing" or "I did it my way," convey the philosophy of intense independence. But the truth of the matter is that there is no such thing as a totally independent person. John Donne said: in his "Meditation" "No man is an island, entire of itself,/Everyone is a piece of the continent, a part of the main."

Another reason we find it difficult to be cooperative is that we are highly competitive. All the way from sibling rivalry to a sports mad culture, to an economic system based on competition, we are taught to be competitive. We are told again and again to be number one, that winning is everything and that nobody remembers who comes in second. Yet Jesus Christ, the Son of God, "made himself of no reputation, and took upon him the form of a servant, . . . he humbled himself, . . . unto death" (Phil. 2:7-8). He was, in the standards of the world, a loser.

Yet as difficult as it is for us to cooperate, the nature of the gospel demands it. All believers are one in Jesus Christ and that is the foundation of the church. There is one Lord, one faith, one baptism. The beautiful word *fellowship* in the Greek, *koinonia,* means "partnership." Jesus prayed the night before he died that all believers would be one so that the world might believe in him. The book of Acts records the advance of the early church, part of which was the result of a unity in the Spirit. Cooperation is woven into the fabric of God's redemptive plan.

Now cooperation does not mean compromise. In order for Christians to cooperate with one another to extend God's kingdom, we don't have to compromise our convictions or our identity. Nor must churches relinquish their autonomous independence in order to cooperate with other churches. The reason for this is that the basis of our cooperation is the lordship of Jesus Christ. Because Jesus is our Lord, we each follow him; we each listen to his Spirit; we each obey his Word. This means that, in his own beautiful and perfect way, he knits lives together without violating our individual identities and responsibilities. Cooperation under the lordship of Christ does not mean compromise. It means unity. It is not a sign of weakness. Rather it is a sign of strength and solidarity.

Of all the churches to which the apostle Paul wrote letters, none showed more fragmentation and more division than the Corinthian church. In our text he called them "babes in Christ" and "carnal" because of their envyings, strife, and division. Against this background the apostle said, "We are labourers together with God." Urging the Corinthians to resist a competitive devisiveness he teaches some very important truths about being co-workers with each other and with God in the extension of his Kingdom. And as he does Paul gives us some theological principles that are the basis of the way we as Southern Baptists finance our world mission enterprise.

First, cooperation requires independent responsibility. Each and every person is important to God. Each and every believer is important in God's plan for world redemption. He calls each of us. He equips each of us. He places each of us. There's no such thing as a Christian that doesn't fit into God's strategy. Paul asked, "Who is Paul? Who is Apollos?" (v. 5). Then he answered, We are "ministers by whom you believed, . . . I have planted, Apollos watered" (vv. 5-6). What he was saying is that God calls and equips each to a certain task. Each has individual responsibility, and it is important for each to fulfill those responsibilities.

The first lesson to be learned in teamwork is the crucial necessity of each team member doing his job. In the Dallas-Green Bay game for the NFL championship, in what is called the Ice Bowl, there is an interesting story. Green Bay was behind but had the ball on the Dallas one-foot line with very little time to go. In the huddle before that fourth-down play, Bart Star, the quarterback, said to Jerry Kramer, "You move that man in front of you twelve inches, and you'll make $15,000." There never has been and there never will be a substitute for an individual member of a team doing his job.

In similar fashion there can be no substitute for individual Christians accepting independently the responsibility God gives to them. There will never be any authentic cooperation until we learn to say what Isaiah said, "Here am I, Lord, send me." Or to say what Paul said, "What wilt thou have me to do?"

And just as individuals must accept independent responsibility, so must churches. There can be no substitute for churches that seek to fulfill the Great Commission where they are located. Nothing can take the place of churches which believe God has put them in their community to be like leaven, salt, and light. A local, functioning fellowship of believers is still God's strategy for world redemption. When we as churches come to the place when we are willing to do whatever God wants us to do, to pray, to work, to witness, then we've taken the first step in cooperating with God and cooperating with others in extending Christ's kingdom.

But cooperation requires more than individuals and churches accepting their independent responsibilities. *It also requires interdependent unity with one another.* Verse 8 says, "Now he that planteth and he that watereth are one." Using an agricultural analogy the text shows how Christians must depend on each other and work together. If no one planted, the watering would be useless. If no one watered, the planting would be useless. Each fulfilling independent responsibility must recognize the necessity and importance of others fulfilling their responsibility. We are linked together; therefore, we must serve together, pray together, and work together.

Interdependent unity means we recognize our need of each other. Interdependent unity means we respect each other's gifts, calling, and commitment. Interdependent unity means we rejoice in each other's victories and weep over each other's defeats. Interdependent unity means we renew communication with each other and refresh each other with support, encouragement, and prayer.

In praying for each other we demonstrate our interdependent unity. It's difficult to pray for someone and feel isolated from him. How you pray probably tells you how much you feel tied to others in a spirit of cooperation. If all you do is pray for yourself—your ministry, your church, your class, your needs—probably you haven't realized the importance of interdependent unity. Nothing would tie us together as churches like intercessory prayer for each other. Nothing would tie us together even within our churches like intercessory prayer for each other.

Also in financially supporting world missions we demonstrate our interdependent unity. The Cooperative Program is a proven vehicle for that support. How a church participates in world missions tells a great deal about that church's feeling of unity with other churches. How much a church gives to extend Christ's kingdom beyond its own city reveals the extent of that church's vision. If all your church does is build, witness, and work in its locale, it hasn't realized the importance of interdependent unity with other churches.

When a church makes bold commitment to world mission giving, she is showing her compassion for the whole world. She is declaring her unity in purpose and Spirit with other churches. And most important, she will accomplish far more in the extension of Christ's kingdom than she could by herself.

There's one more ingredient in cooperation. It requires dependent reliance on God. Verse 7, "So then neither is he that planteth any thing; neither he that watereth; but God that giveth the increase." Using an agricultural analogy the text shows how the farmer has the privilege of participating in a very exciting venture. One plants seed. Another waters. But then they must wait, and only God can cause the seed to grow. We who fulfill independent responsibility and practice interdependent unity with others are absolutely dependent upon the sovereign power of God. Only God can save a soul. Only God can quicken a conscience. Only God can renew a spirit. Only God can redeem a life. And we are totally dependent on him to do it.

The kingdom belongs to God. And his kingdom will be triumphant with or without us. The day will come when his glory will cover the earth like waters cover the sea, regardless of what we do. But in his great grace and love God has given us the blessed privilege of participating with him in the extension of his kingdom. He has allowed us to cooperate with him, to be participants with him. This entire business of cooperation with others and with God is not a regimen. It's a romance. It's not just a doctrine. It's an adventure.

Let's join in it, *together.*

Albert McClellan is associate executive secretary and director of program planning for the Executive Committee of the Southern Baptist Convention, having served as a member of the Executive Committee staff since 1959. He is a native of Bowie, Texas, and is a graduate of Southwestern Baptist Theological Seminary.

15

THE MISSIONARY FUTURE OF THE CHURCH

Psalm 22:27-31

The right of a God of love to rule all people everywhere in all time is the supreme motivation for missions. When Jesus said, "Go therefore and make disciples of all nations . . . lo, I am with you always, to the close of the age" (Matt. 28:19-20, RSV), he was declaring the sovereignty of God both in space and in time. When he said, "God so loved the world" (John 3:16), he was making clear the divine right of missions.

Since William Carey went to India in 1792, God's modern-day

missionaries have been moving forward into new vistas of geography and new reaches of time to bring the good news that "in Christ God was reconciling the world to himself" (2 Cor. 5:19, RSV). The spirit of this movement can be seen in a letter written by a Baptist missionary. "For five miles the frame of my car dragged bottom and for a good twenty miles I was unable to shift out of the first two gears. We then widened the footpath by bowling over some small trees and began to walk to the small village which we could see in the distance."

Like William Carey, this missionary did not know what lay ahead, only that "God so loved the world . . . " (John 3:16). He knew God loved not part of the world but all of it, the last man, the last woman, and the last child in most distant time. The true missionary goes the whole distance because he knows that Jesus Christ "is the expiation for our sins, and not for ours only but also for the sins of the whole world" (1 John 2:2, RSV). He also knows that the sovereignty of God is proved by the grace of God, and that only a God of redemptive love could give himself as the expiation of man's iniquities. The missionary experience begins with the acceptance of a loving God as sovereign in the whole world.

This view of missions speaks to the permanence and the vitality of the church. We know that Jesus Christ committed the gospel to the church and "that through the church the manifold wisdom of God might now be made known to the principalities and powers in the heavenly places" (Eph. 3:10, RSV). The church indeed does have a future. There was no doubt of this in the mind of Jesus. He looked ahead and said, "The powers of death shall not prevail against it" (Matt. 16:18, RSV). Paul too believed in the future of the church. He said, "To him be glory in the church by Christ Jesus throughout all ages, world without end" (Eph. 3:21). The Great Commission was given to last unto the end of the world. It derived from God's absolute authority over all mankind, an authority made clear on almost every page of the Scriptures.

One clear passage is Psalm 22:27-31 in which there are two compelling phrases: "dominion belongs to the Lord" (v. 28, RSV) and "posterity shall serve him" (v. 30, RSV). These speak of God's supreme universality and God's imminent timeliness. The church should take heed and prepare for the future, for the future is almost here.

Dominion Belongs to the Lord

"Dominion" comes from a family of words that include *dominant* and *dominate*. The phrase simply means that authority belongs to God. No nation can effectively pass laws against him, no people can shut him out of their future, and no other kingdom can close its doors to him because ultimately and absolutely he is the ruler. He is the highest and the best, the God of love before whom all must bow and the God of justice before whom all must stand in judgment.

As the church contemplates her future, she can take assurance that wherever she goes in the world or in the future, she has the right to be there. Before the church arrives, God has already established his sovereignty.

He did this through Jesus Christ who is "the true light that enlightens every man" (John 1:9, RSV) and who entered the world of mankind. No matter where the church goes, God's presence has already spoken through Jesus Christ. His sovereignty precedes all missionaries to all fields in all time. "Dominion belongs to the Lord" (Ps. 22:28, RSV).

Because of his dominion great things happen. For one, "All the ends of the earth shall remember" (Ps. 22:27, RSV). In a day such as ours when much of the world forgets, some find it hard to believe there will come a time when all the world will remember. The floods of ungodliness are everywhere, and they make some of us afraid. Too often despair seizes ministers and hopelessness paralyzes churches. For such Christians the psalmist's words are good medicine. Take courage, you discouraged and frightened people, dominion belongs to the Lord. He rules the nations and the people indeed will remember.

One cannot read the Old Testament without the feeling of God's rule over all and that he holds dominion over history as well as over nations. He is actively concerned with what happens to man. He will not indefinitely tolerate indifference and rebellion. "God is a righteous judge, and a God who has indignation every day. If a man does not repent, God will whet his sword" (Ps. 7:11-12, RSV).

Not only will the people remember, they will "turn to the Lord" (Ps. 22:27, RSV). The invincible Christ will conquer every human heart. Finally the people will hear and believe.

As Baptists press toward a goal of witnessing to every person by the year 2000, they can be assured that someday in some way "the ends of the earth will remember and turn to the Lord." Who knows? It could be by the end of this century. The same Spirit that brooded over the face of the earth in creation broods again over the new creation. Because of his awakening, the people will remember and believe.

If not this century, then the century to come, or the one after that, or the next one—surely someday. The promise is given. Until then the church has a future as Christ's husbandman to help him work in his vineyard of all humanity everywhere in space and time.

Further, because of his sovereignty, "all the families of the nations shall worship before him" (Ps. 22:27, RSV). All families of all nations! When Jesus said, "The field is the world" (Matt. 13:38, RSV), he surely meant every person. The Lord spoke to Isaiah: "To me every knee shall bow, every tongue shall swear" (Isa. 45:23, RSV). Paul repeated the promise: "Every knee shall bow . . . every tongue shall give praise" (Rom. 14:11, RSV).

John's Patmos vision of God's triumph shows us a Lord totally the conqueror. "The kingdom of the world has become the kingdom of our Lord and of his Christ, and he shall reign for ever and ever" (Rev. 11:15, RSV). John saw a great multitude that no man could number. The people came as worshipers from every nation, every tribe, every family, every tongue, and every temperament. "The proud of the earth shall bow down" (Ps. 22:29, RSV), and even the dying shall bow down. They will bow to a God who loves them as much as himself, a God of mercy who forgives their sins, and a God of renewal who transforms their lives.

No wonder that long ago in London, England, when Handel presented his oratorio, *The Messiah,* King George II spontaneously stood when the Hallelujah Chorus was sung. He could not restrain himself in the presence of a Savior so magnificent. He stood because in his heart he had already bowed.

Most of us see the world of the present. We scarcely remember that just as before we existed there were believers, after us too will be believers, but not the psalmist. He was a futurist of magnificent vision. He saw the triumph of God over the hearts of men and said, "Posterity shall serve him" (Ps. 22:30, RSV).

Posterity Shall Serve Him

Many people in these revolutionary times wonder about the future of the church. They are discouraged by its temporary setbacks. Some even relate the church to its material welfare. If it is prosperous, they conclude the church is succeeding, and if it is poor the church is failing. Others see the moral and spiritual decadence of American urban culture and say, "Surely the church is dying." A few of these detractors are themselves church members; because of their own spiritual decay, they shed tears of defeat, but not tears of regret. This poor vision of the church of tomorrow is more related to their own vulnerability than it is to God's invulnerability. They do not see themselves as either the objects or the means of Christ's great mission to the ends of the earth. For them the church is merely something joined, not a life commitment or a life-style; a membership, not a fellowship; an organization, not a mission.

A true soldier gives his life gloriously with the assurance that though he pays the highest personal sacrifice, the war ultimately will be won. Even if the war is not won, the cause itself is worth the cost. Not so the church member without a missionary vision of the future. For him the cause is already lost, especially if the work of the church goes badly or if his own efforts are fruitless or if he cannot measure the church's labor by worldly standards. He simply does not grasp that Christianity itself is a mission to the whole world and that its calendar includes the future.

The church indeed does have a future but only if she remains faithful to Christ's world mission. And again what is that mission? It is that all people everywhere and in all time to come shall be "fellow heirs, members of the same body, and partakers of the promise in Christ Jesus through the gospel" (Eph. 3:6, RSV). This is the narrow way of which Jesus spoke, the one that leads to life. It is so narrow that it excludes all philosophies and creeds and concentrates solely on the awesome fact that "God shows his love for us in that while we were yet sinners Christ died for us" (Rom. 5:8, RSV). This narrow truth offers far more to the world than merely meeting humanity's need. God's purpose in Christ and man's human needs do not exclude each other, for God's love is given for man's need. But unless God's people on mission start from God's purpose, they soon lose the vision. The person who doubts the future of the church almost certainly has his eyes more on the human than on the divine. He surely does not remember, "Posterity shall serve him" (Ps. 22:30, RSV).

For the church to remain faithful to Christ's world mission, she must learn again how to effectively evangelize. If missions is the strategic approach to her task, evangelization is the tactical approach. God's sovereignty establishes the church's right to evangelize; Christ's commandment establishes the church's duty to evangelize, and the Holy Spirit's presence establishes her power to evangelize. Psalm 22:27-31 clearly establishes some of the effect of God's movement in the future, and at the forefront of that movement is evangelization.

For one thing, "Men shall tell of the Lord" (Ps. 22:30, RSV). The Word of God will not die because the Holy Spirit will not die. He is the bridge of the ages, the great connection of past, present, and future. Because of him men will always be telling of the Lord "to the coming generation" (Ps. 22:30, RSV) and "to a people yet unborn" (Ps. 22:31, RSV). In the power of the Spirit they will speak the Word and the people will hear and will be saved. There will be periods of sowing and periods of reaping, but in the end the harvest will come.

Telling the gospel is more than the tradition of the church. It is part of the church's mandate. Jesus said, "Teaching them to observe all that I have commanded you" (Matt. 28:20, RSV). Along with ministry, telling is the life and mission of the church. Without forceful telling, the church is not really the church. The power of the telling is the presence of God's Spirit in the life of the teller and in the action of Jesus Christ in the heart of the one told. "And how are they to hear without a preacher? And how can men preach unless they are sent? So faith comes from what is heard, and what is heard comes by the preaching of Christ" (Rom. 10:14,15,17, RSV). Teaching or preaching, the church's telling must always be of the crucified and risen Lord. It is not of ourselves we tell, not our devotion, not our creeds, and not our works. It is what God has done in Christ—God's love, God's grace, God's gift, God's salvation, God's victory! It is not a mere telling that man can be saved but that God in Christ can save him. The telling of the church is the oral confession of the cross of Christ in its application to all men everywhere and in all of time. To proclaim Jesus Christ is to help claim the sovereignty of God for all men. As long as this task stands, there is work for the church to do, and the gates of death shall not prevail against it.

God's movement into the future means to "proclaim his deliverance" (Ps. 22:31, RSV). Not merely a story is told but a special story of deliverance and that God "has wrought it" (Ps. 22:31, RSV).

The story of deliverance runs through the whole Bible. In the Old Testament Adam and Eve outside the gate of Eden were promised deliverance. Abraham was delivered from his enemies and Lot from burning Sodom. Israel was delivered from slavery in Egypt and Daniel from the lion's den. In the New Testament lepers were delivered from their disease, blind men from blindness, and sinners from their sins. The crowning act of deliverance was wrought by Jesus on the cross. His death made man free, free of their sins, free of their guilt, free of slavery to the law, free of their fears, free of themselves, and free of death. This is a glorious deliverance. "For freedom Christ has set us free; stand fast therefore, and do not submit again to a yoke of slavery" (Gal. 5:1, RSV). As long as men are enslaved to their sins and themselves, the church will have work to do—the high and holy work of deliverance.

The good news of deliverance will be the task of the church of tomorrow. Deliverance will always be the content of the church's telling. If the Baptist purpose to witness to all the people in the world by the year 2000 seems too visionary, and if it seems specious to plan to preach to souls yet unborn, then let it be remembered that because deliverance is preached "posterity shall serve him." As long as God reigns, he shall be sovereign for all men everywhere and in all time. And as long as the church has a future, she has the obligation to claim that future in the name of the Lord. The church will surely know that whatever she accomplishes it is God who "has wrought it."

The presence of God as the working power of the church must never be overlooked. The secret of successful mission is that God works ahead of us both in geography and time. Jesus put it plainly, "My Father is working still, and I am working" (John 5:17, RSV). The church as the body of Christ is to continue God's work on earth, knowing that wherever she goes, God goes ahead of her and with her. There is no corner of this world where God has not already laid his claim. There is no moment of present or future time when God is not already present. He opens the way for us to do our work. "He who believes in me will also do the works that I do; and greater works will he do, because I go to the Father" (John 14:12, RSV). As we work at his world mission task, God's Spirit works in us to give us the victory.

The church's commitment to missions can be both reluctant and irrevocable. Reluctant in that she comes slowly to see the world as her true field. The needs at home, the remoteness of the far corners of the earth, the uncertainty of the future in strange lands, the lack of tangible evidence of the effect of her mission work abroad—all this contributes to the church's reluctance. But once the decision is made and the church enters joyously into the world mission task, she becomes keenly aware of God's sovereign presence in far away lands. Suddenly her commitment to missions is irrevocable.

A traveler paused in Mexico City to ask about the highway to the Caribbean coast. He was afraid that an earthquake a month before had left the roads impossible to travel. The man in the tour office assured the traveler that everything was fine. When the traveler showed reluctance, the man simply said, "People live there too." That assurance eased the traveler's burden. Churches and missionaries have been often comforted with the assurance that no matter how torn the mission field, God lives there too. Once that truth is accepted, the missions commitment becomes irrevocable. The church must do her work wherever she believes God to be.

A young lady began feeling she should become a missionary, much against her wish and her will. Even after she married a minister and he heard the mission call, she strongly resisted the idea of becoming a missionary, knowing all the time God was calling her. Her frequent prayers, "Please, Lord, don't send me" went unanswered and she became a missionary. Gradually she came to full commitment. It was a reluctant journey but one conditioned by a conviction of God's universal sovereignty. At the end of her first furlough it appeared that she might not be able to return to the mission field. She said it was a feeling of terrifying emptiness. She prayed "Please Lord, let me go." She had come the full distance. Her reluctance had become an irrevocable commitment. So with many a church, slow at first to see Christ's world mission, once dedicated to it, that mission becomes her life—all because God surely reigns wherever people live, and he reigns tomorrow as he reigns today. It is the promise of his universal kingdom that draws us irrevocably to missions.

R. Keith Parks has served as the executive
director of the Foreign Mission Board of the
Southern Baptist Convention since January 1,
1980. He is a native of Memphis, Texas, and a
graduate of Southwestern Baptist Theological
Seminary.

16
THE HUMANITY-WIDE CALL

John 12:20-36

Apprentice Buddhist monks leaned forward, eyes glinting with
expectancy. It was missionary Jerry Perrill's daily Bible study time
in the largest Buddhist temple in Vientiane, Laos. These brilliant
young men had honed their minds through daily study since the
age of thirteen. In their late twenties, they now had command of
several languages, philosophical concepts and world religions,
among other disciplines. They were the graduate students of the
"Buddhist seminaries."

Finally their leader looked carefully into my eyes: "Sir, we search for God in our religion, but we cannot find him. Can you help us find God?" Before the answer came, another student hurriedly added, "It's as though God is across the Mekong River. We have no boat; there's no bridge; we can't swim. Can you help us across the Mekong to where God is?"

"Yes," I replied. "This Bible you have studied with the missionary shows you the way. The way is Jesus Christ."

As we walked away, we felt that perhaps "Saul of Vientiane" might be in that group. But the Communists came, and the missionaries had to leave. Although other Buddhist monks have found God in Jesus Christ, I do not know what happened to these young men.

These religious leaders calling out for God represent multitudes. There are more people seeking the true God today than at any time in human history. From every part of our world, although not in every country, there are more people to be won than ever. Many are like a Maasi young woman. Missionary Harold Cummins wondered why her people were responding now but had not in the past. It was not a resistance to the gospel, she declared. It was simply that no one had told them about Jesus. Untold millions have not heard. Multitudes among them would respond. But, there is no one to tell them.

However, "The Humanity-wide Call" is not based simply on the cry of lost people from all over the world. Its foundation goes deeper than man's need and is older than man's existence. It is found in the heart of God. His love is humanity wide—as is his call to us.

The Source of This Call

Certain Greeks wanted to see Jesus. Why did they ask Philip? Crowds constantly thronged around Jesus. Why didn't they go to him directly? Why was the coming of the Greeks different?

Jesus' response reveals his startling assessment. Their coming meant the purpose of his earthly mission had reached its peak. His hour had come. He was to be glorified (v. 23), and his Father's name was to be glorified (v. 28). This meant that the tarnish built up through years of traditional Jewish misconceptions would be cleansed by the scouring of the crucifixion and the polishing of the resurrection.

God emphasized from the beginning that his purpose was to save all humanity (Gen. 12:3). The Jews had difficulty believing that their Messiah was for all people. If others would become Jews, then they could share in their religion. Tragically, some Americans seem to feel Jesus' primary reason for coming was for Americans.

The Greeks came. Jesus said this indicated that his coming was finding fulfillment. Said he, "And I, if I be lifted up from the earth, will draw all men unto me" (John 12:32). This, plus many other passages, says his authority is over all people; his redemption is for everyone. Thus, anyone who calls Jesus Lord, yet limits personal concern and commitment to less than the whole of humanity, stands in conflict with Jesus.

The Nature of This Call

This passage is a clarion call to follow Christ. It is a call to a life-style of death. Self must be crossed out. Jesus looked through these Greeks to all nations of all ages. He yearned for the salvation of us all. But even as he saw our need, he blurted out his own anguish. The turmoil of his soul underscored his awareness of the costly nature of this call (John 12:27). Yet this was the very reason he had come to live among us (John 1:14). He would not recoil from his mission. His passion was to reveal the true nature of God's love to all humanity. This only could be done through the crucifixion kind of death he faced.

His vision extended to the extremities of the race, and beyond time and physical realities. His calling, and ours, is to spiritual combat because of Satan's power over sinful man. God's righteous judgment on sin includes the destruction of the one who rules over the sinful. The certainty that Satan's power would be broken makes Christ's cross into a throne (John 12:31-33). The shout of triumph, "It is finished" (John 19:30), was the claiming of victory.

Christ has never called anyone to any sacrifice that he was not willing to make. He clearly stated that unless we are willing to die, we cannot live. He does not sugarcoat his call with syrupy piousity or blur it by dimming the light of truth or express it diplomatically in the vagueness of ecclesiastical rhetoric. He said simply: "A seed must die to bear fruit—or it remains a barren single seed" (John 12:24, author's paraphrase).

To put one's own life in first place is to lose all. To voluntarily renounce all claim to self and the world is to find eternal life and the kingdom.

This call to win "the Greeks" is not only the call to sacrifice and death but also the call to victory and life. To hoard and hold for self results in loneliness, unfruitfulness, selfishness, and sinfulness. To serve him is to follow him to the cross—and to eternal victory. Paul, who lived out this calling to preach the gospel to the Greeks better than anyone other than Jesus, echoed this concept (read Phil. 3:10-11).

The call is individual. Jesus speaks of a seed and of one life. The call is very personal. No one can make this choice or perform this task for anyone else. The call is thrilling. Jesus speaks of multiplying oneself many times as "much fruit" is promised. The results are neither for a season nor a lifetime. They are for eternity.

The Greeks came immediately following the triumphal entry. With shouts of celebration and waving of palm branches, the crowds were proclaiming Jesus the Messiah. After Christ clarified what fellowship really meant, they renounced, rejected, and reviled him (John 12:37-50). This call to go to all mankind cannot be fulfilled merely by glorious celebrations. The crowds shouting for deliverance and the urging to kingship were prompted by self-interest. In current terms this might mean:

—Believing that going to exciting and enjoyable religious meetings fulfills Christian obligations.

—Holding as criterion for religious activity, what do I get out of it?

—Feeling that emphasis on service, sacrifice, discipleship, and giving (especially tithing) justifies joining some less demanding group.

We Christians need to learn that Christianity does not find its finest expression in moments of exhilaration, palm branch waving, worship, and the shouting of hosannahs. Not long ago I heard one of our missionaries, Webster Carroll, who spent eight years under the dictatorship of Idi Amin in Uganda. The Carrolls and the Jim Rices were in and out of that country during all that time. Web reported that during those tense days a Ugandan Baptist pastor said to him, "I want to give you a report from our church."

Web said, "Our denomination is banned. You must not meet."

The pastor said, "Oh, that's not what I mean. We are not meeting, but the church is active in Uganda. On one day of the week I'll say to these two church members, 'Tomorrow you walk down this street. Read your Bible and sing your hymns. If people want to know, tell them about Jesus.' I'll say to these two, 'You go to the bus station and sit there and sing hymns and read Scripture, and as people are interested, come back to tell me.' Tomorrow I will send another couple down there. It would be dangerous to send the same people to the same place each day. Here is the report of our church as it has been walking the streets and bearing witness among the people of Uganda."

That's what Jesus was talking about when the Greeks came. He said the time had come to understand what Christianity is all about. It gives itself in the market place to people in need. The Greeks, the nations, are calling our churches out into their market place. Their call is urgent.

The Urgency of This Call

Jesus underscored this urgency. Judgment is *now.* The light will remain only a while longer. Darkness comes. Those in darkness do not know where they're going. Jesus urges belief because he knows people are lost and desperate. Today many question this.

Let's put this question frankly: Do you believe that a loving God will send people to hell who have never heard about Jesus? Do you believe people who have never heard are lost? Let me answer succinctly. This is not the proper question if the Bible is true when it says: "The soul that sinneth, it shall die" (Ezek. 18:4); "The wages of sin is death" (Rom. 6:23); "There is none righteous, no not one" (Rom. 3:10); "All have sinned, and come short of the

glory of God" (Rom. 3:23). The Bible never says that if you have
sinned but have never heard about Jesus, you are all right. The
Bible says sin has separated man from God and any living soul
cursed by sin is doomed forever.

But that's not fair, you say. That's right. The Bible never said it
was fair. When my wife and I went to Indonesia as missionaries,
we took one son; during our period of time there, three other
children were born into our family. When we came home on our
first furlough, the son born during that first term, although he
appeared healthy, was diagnosed as having tuberculosis. In
Indonesia we had buried young and old, babe and grandfather,
because of tuberculosis. It was one of the prime killers in Indonesia. We thought his death warrant had been sealed. The doctor
treating him said, "Oh no, there are three medicines that destroy
the tuberculin germ." For more than two years we gave him two of
those medicines. The germ was destroyed and he lived.

It isn't fair that multiplied thousands die every year from the
same germ that the right medicines can kill. It isn't fair that my
son, because of the circumstances and finances of his parents,
could receive the medicine to kill the germ in his body, and he
could live. Of course, it is unfair. But that tuberculin germ does
not consider fairness. It acts according to its nature; unless it is
destroyed, it destroys the body it infects.

Sin is like that. Sin is destroyed only when it comes in contact
with the divine remedy, Jesus Christ, who alone can destroy sin.
"The soul that sinneth, it will die" (Ezek. 18:4). Whether the
sinner knows about it or not, he is separated from God and condemned. Please read carefully. The loving God I know is not in the
business of sending anybody to hell. But those who are in sin are
already condemned to hell. God in heaven poured out his most
precious possession, gave his only begotten Son. That Son came
and died on a cross in order that those who are already condemned
to hell could be redeemed. God is doing all he can do to save a
world already condemned. And whenever a person is saved, Christ
says to that one, "Just as my Father hath sent me, even so send I
you" (John 20:21). Whenever one of us is saved, we are sent on
the mission to redeem the world from the sin in which that world

already lives. This, then, is the question for those of us who claim we love God with all of our heart, mind, soul, and body: Will we allow the rest of the world to remain under condemnation because we don't care enough to tell them about Jesus?

The eager responsiveness of so many lost people emphasizes this urgency. Multitudes are responding, and other multitudes await.

The Sukuma people of Tanzania demonstrated this fact. In the summer of 1979 the Baptists there sent out 7 evangelistic teams which started 56 new congregations in 8 weeks. The two-man teams baptized 2,575 people in villages where Baptists had no previous witness.

In Manila, missionary Howard Olive preached in a large auditorium. Many persons were saved. Thirty-eight stood in line to request that he come to start churches in their homes or shops or other places. Howard's schedule already overflowed. To those wanting to hear the gospel, the solution was obvious: Send us someone else. The answer was likewise simple—and tragic: There is no one else to send. The Greeks cry out for someone to tell them of Jesus.

The Scope of This Call

Christ issues the call to every believer: "As my Father hath sent me, even so send I you" (John 20:21). The call comes also to each church. In Matthew 16 Jesus tells us that his church, with heavenly orders and power, will storm through the gates of hell. Each Christian and each church is responsible to do everything possible to share Christ with all humanity. Each of us is saved and each church is born with that purpose.

The Greeks have come. What then shall we say? "Father, don't make us be your witnesses. Deliver us from this responsibility." It was for this responsibility that we are saved. What then must we say? "Father, glorify yourself in us, as we give you our lives in order that the peoples of the world might know Jesus."

This giving of life will probably not be as one of our missionaries. In May 1978 Archie Dunaway, a veteran missionary at the Sanyati Hospital in Rhodesia, was brutally bayoneted to death. A little later, the only remaining missionary doctor, Maurice

Randall, though relocated in a city, continued going periodically to the hospital, on irregular schedules, to minister to the rural people. Davis Saunders, the area secretary, asked, "Will you close the hospital?"

"Oh no," said the doctor. "If the hospital is closed, more people will die than will die if we keep it open."

Davis looked at Shirley and Maurice Randall, thought of their two small children, and asked, "Do you realize the risk you run in keeping the hospital open?"

Shirley replied, "We understand the risk. But we believe there are still some things worth dying for."

The nations call. Do we believe they are worth dying for? What would it take to tell the world about Jesus? We have said as Southern Baptists that we are going to have our part in that. What will it require?

It will take much more than we have yet done. On the average, we as Southern Baptists give through the Cooperative Program less than 3½ percent of our undesignated money to reach out beyond the United States to win nearly 95 percent of the world. As Southern Baptists we give $4.80 per person per year to win the people outside the United States to Jesus Christ.

We will not tell the world about Jesus until we are willing to deprive ourselves of some of the things that money will buy and give sacrificially beyond our church and beyond our state and beyond our nation in order that "the Greeks" who are calling out for Jesus might know about him.

We will not win them until more among us become willing to give their lives to go out to share the gospel. In 1978, as Southern Baptists, we appointed 350 missionaries, more than ever before. In 1979 the requests for new missionaries from the 95 countries where you have missionaries added up to 1,526 more missionaries. In 1978 it took 100,000 of us to find one to go as a career missionary. In that same year, as in the years previous, of those graduating from our seminaries, 95 percent said, "We'll stay here," and only 5 percent said, "We will go yonder where almost 95 percent of the world's population lives." We will never win the world or have our appropriate place in fulfilling our spiritual calling with responses like that. As churches and as individuals we must become so burdened for the world that we join in earnest daily prayer saying, "Lord God, thrust out laborers into your harvest fields in order that the world might know about Jesus."

It will cost. But it will cost more not to do it. Some years ago in Orlando, Florida, Mr. and Mrs. Graham Walker had been struggling with God's call to mission service. They had come to feel that they could not go because he had not been able to sell his business. A place in Singapore needed a business manager, a treasurer, and Graham filled the qualifications. But time was running out because of the ages of their four children. The deadline came and Graham called Richmond and said, "We couldn't make the arrangements; we can't go."

Jeannie took two aspirin and went to sleep. Graham took two aspirin, and "they bounced like Ping-Pong balls in my stomach," he said. He paced the floor and wrestled with God. He bargained: "God, I can't go. But I'll give my influence, and this will be the most mission-minded church in the world."

It was as though God spoke, "Graham, what will you tell people in that church when they talk about going to the mission field if you don't go?"

Graham tried again. "God, I teach a group of young men. I'll pour my life into them."

And again he heard, "Graham, what will you tell them when they talk about vocational choices and God's will?"

Said Graham, "I've got four children and my wife. I'm going to be a better Christian father and husband than I have ever been."

Came the reply, "And what will you tell your sons and daughters when they begin talking about life's vocations?"

At 2:00 AM, Graham Walker called Louis Cobbs, personnel secretary at the Foreign Mission Board, and said, "If that position I turned down at 5:00 last night hasn't been filled, I want to go." It was still open. Then Graham said, "It was costing me more to stay than it would cost me to go because it was costing me my Christian witness."

I'm not saying God has called all of you to be missionaries. I am saying he has called more Southern Baptists to be missionaries

than have heard him. I am saying he is calling all of us to die to self
and to accept his will for our lives.

Some might say, "If God would tell me what his will is, then I'd
let him know if I'd do it." God doesn't act that way. When my
children say, "Daddy, will you promise to do something?" I say
no. I understand they are about to ask something they know I
wouldn't agree to if I knew first what it was. But God comes on
those terms. He says, "Will you do what I ask you to do?" When
you reply "Tell me what it is first," he knows you are not ready to
do it. Jesus said in John 7:17: "If any man's will is to do his will,
he shall know whether the teaching is from God or whether I am
speaking on my own authority" (RSV).

The simple question comes first: Are you willing to do his will?
After you say yes, then God will say, "Here is what it is." Some
can't find his will because they say, "Show me first; then I'll
decide." God says, "Die first to self; then I'll tell you what my will
is."

The hour has come. Shall I say, "Father, don't let me make this
decision"?

"But it was for this hour that you came into the world," replies
God.

"But it will cost me." That's right. It's going to cost your life.
To say no will cost your witness.

Harold C. Bennett has served as the executive secretary-treasurer of the Executive Committee of the Southern Baptist Convention since August 1, 1979. He is a native of Asheville, North Carolina, and a graduate of Southern Baptist Theological Seminary.

17
MARCHING FORWARD UNDER GOD'S ORDERS

Joshua 3:9-17

Congregations and groups of Christians have sung the old hymn, "We've a Story to Tell" by H. Ernest Nichol (1896), with quiet and determined devotion for years. In churches, as well as in great convocations, we have joined our voices with other Christians in boldly singing:

> We've a message to give to the nations,
> That the Lord who reigneth above
> Hath sent us his Son to save us,

And show us that God is love,
And show us that God is love.

For the darkness shall turn to the dawning,
And the dawning to noon-day bright,
And Christ's great kingdom shall come on earth,
The Kingdom of Love and Light.

The task is not yet done. We still have a message to give to the nations.

Yet, it is a convicting truth that not all of the nations of the world have even heard the gospel. More important is the fact that the people of the approximately 212 nations of the world have not responded in faith to Christ.

The assignment from our Lord is clear. We are to go and teach all nations that Jesus Christ is the Son of God and the Savior of the world (Matt. 28:19-20). God has a plan but it requires the personal involvement of all of God's people.

Our home in Florida was in a community where a number of Jewish families lived. Some of these Jewish families are now our close friends. Over the years, we shared with each other and learned to love and respect one another. Although we have moved, we still have a Christian concern for them.

On several occasions, my wife and I were invited to be present for the Bar Mitzvah of one of our friend's children. This is the time when a Jewish boy, at the age of thirteen, becomes responsible and accepts his personal religious duties. The service is an impressive and memorable one. On one such occasion, my wife and I were present for the Bar Mitzvah for our across-the-street neighbor. In the large synagogue, full almost to capacity, he read the Scriptures in Hebrew with clarity and enthusiasm. Then came the time for him to deliver his message to the congregation. He chose to speak about the family. A sentence captured my imagination. He said, "It takes only a moment to become a parent, but it requires a great deal to be a parent."

This thirteen-year-old lad had hit upon a significant truth. As the service continued, at times in Hebrew, and then in English, I let my mind draw a parallel to Christianity. We were probably the only Christians in that great congregation. I had a burden for them. I thought, "It only takes a moment to become a Christian, but it requires a lifetime to be a Christian."

As followers of Jesus Christ, we have accepted salvation through personal faith in Christ. We are now in the process of carrying out the Great Commission our Lord gave us. God has a plan and we must follow his orders if we are to accomplish in our lifetimes what he has in mind for us to do.

God's Man for the Hour

As is recorded in Deuteronomy 31, Joshua was chosen to be the successor to Moses as the leader of Israel, the people of God. Before Moses died, he called Joshua before him in the sight of all Israel and said, "Be strong and of a good courage: for thou must go with this people unto the land which the Lord hath sworn unto their fathers to give them" (Deut. 31:7).

Joshua was a unique follower of God and a dedicated leader of God's people. The Bible portrays him as being almost a second Moses. He cast a mighty shadow over the history of Israel.

The book of Joshua records the miraculous crossing of the Jordan River into the Promised Land. God said to Joshua, "Moses my servant is dead; now therefore arise, go over this Jordan, thou, and all this people, unto the land which I do give to them, even to the children of Israel" (Josh. 1:2).

God had a plan and was about to reveal it to his servant Joshua. Chapter 3 records the historical and phenomenal event of the Israelites crossing the Jordan River as the waters were divided. God had told Joshua exactly what to do.

In Joshua 3:9-17, we find the outline of God's instructions and the result of Joshua's obedience. Notice some of the significant phrases from the Scripture text.

"Hear the words of the Lord your God" (v. 9). When Joshua called the people together, he had a clear message from God. He was going to deliver that message to the people. It is an exciting experience to observe the growth of churches where the Word of the Lord is shared in dynamic presentation. When God's preachers have been blessed with a message from the Lord, people will come to hear.

"Hereby ye shall know that the living God is among you" (v. 10). God was about to work a miracle for his people and to deliver them into the Promised Land. By God's act, the people of Israel would know that God was among them. There would be no question as to who had delivered the Israelites. They would be unable to accomplish the feat within their own power. God's power was needed.

"The ark of the covenant . . . passeth over before you" (v. 11). The ark of the covenant was designed for the two stone tablets of the Decalogue, or the Ten Commandments, given to Moses. The ark was also thought of as the visible symbol of the invisible presence of the Lord God. The ark was carried on the shoulders of the Levitical priests.

"As soon as the soles of the feet of the priests that bear the ark of the Lord . . . shall rest in the waters of Jordan" (v. 13). God did not work a miracle until the feet of the priests, bearing the ark of the covenant, were in the Jordan River. Can you imagine the excitement—and, perhaps, fear—in the hearts of the priests as they walked towards the river.

"For Jordan overfloweth all his banks" (v. 15). This was the time of harvest and the Bible records that the Jordan River overflowed its banks during harvesttime. For forty years, the people of God had been wandering in the wilderness. At times, the land was dry and parched and there was not water. Now, they were marching forward under God's orders toward a flooded river. Everything in them must have rebelled at the instructions, but they were determined to follow Joshua because he was following the commands of the Lord. What must have been the thoughts of those priests as they came closer and closer to the flooded river? As soon as "the feet of the priests that bore the ark were dipped in the brim of the water . . . the waters which came down from above stood and rose up upon an heap" (vv. 15-16). A miracle of God was underway!

"The Israelites passed over on dry ground" (v. 17). This was God's victory. By this very act, the Israelites knew that the living God was among them. There was no question but that God had again delivered his people.

Joshua was God's man for the hour. His influence in the lives of the people of God was evident throughout his lifetime. God's people marched forward under God's orders and were successful. The same can be true today.

God Is Looking for Better Men

Although it may not be possible to compare the ministers of today with those of yesteryear, I am confident that there are more qualified, God-called preachers of the gospel today than ever in the history of Christianity. From small churches in the mountain coves of the old South to the great metropolitan complexes of the North and the far West, there are churches served by great men of God. As pastors and church staff members, these men and women are committed to sharing the gospel of Christ with everyone. Yet, there is an urgent need for more and better servants of our Lord.

These dedicated church leaders along with denominational servants have developed programs and projects which challenge the very best within our churches. These methods and programs have evolved over the years and are effective when blessed of God.

Church leaders are always anxious to develop a new thrust or create a new ministry. We should not belittle such efforts, but as leaders we should strive to be better men.

God is looking for better servants to do his bidding. Hanani, the prophet, points clearly to this biblical truth. Second Chronicles 16 records the conflict between Israel, the Northern Kingdom, and Judah, the Southern Kingdom. Baasha, king of Israel, initiated a conflict with Judah. Asa, king of Judah, was in the thirty-sixth year of his reign. Instead of trusting in God, King Asa decided to sign an agreement with Benhadad, king of Syria, who dwelt in Damascus.

Hanani, the prophet of the Lord, had the courage to remind King Asa of God's deliverance in years gone by. Hanani said, "For the eyes of the Lord run to and fro throughout the whole earth, to shew himself strong in the behalf of them whose heart is perfect toward him" (2 Chron. 16:9).

Asa was angry at the prophet and threw him into prison. Nevertheless, the truth of the message of the prophet still stands: God is always looking for better servants through whom he might work in accomplishing his plan to share his love with every person in the world.

Years later, we find another example in Uzziah, when he was king of Judah. He was made king of Judah at the age of sixteen (2 Chron. 26). He did that which was right in the sight of the Lord and God blessed him. His reputation spread far abroad. He became a strong leader.

A change came within his heart: "But when he was strong, his heart was lifted up to his destruction: for he transgressed against the Lord his God, and went into the temple of the Lord to burn incense upon the altar of incense" (2 Chron. 26:16). The priests of the Lord confronted him and charged him with sin against God. King Uzziah was angry with the priests, but God's judgment fell. Uzziah died a leper. You will remember that it was during this year that Isaiah was called into service.

God's preachers and God's leaders must be willing to pay the price to grow spiritually and become channels of blessings to the nations of the world. They must be willing to "take root downward," in order that they may be impowered to "bear fruit upward" (2 Kings 19:30).

Spiritual Need in the World

Those who have eyes to see and ears to hear have no difficulty in recognizing the spiritual needs within our communities, our nation, and the nations of the world. Recently, it was necessary for me to be in New York City for a special conference with some of the executives in the television industry. When I arrived in New York, I watched the local news on television. For a solid hour, the newscaster listed one crisis after another. There was no good news—only a reporting of the crimes and the other tragedies of the day. It was a depressing experience. That city was in spiritual need.

A review of the denominational statistics of the religious bodies reflects a general decline. In many churches, there is no longer an excitement about reaching people for Christ.

Although the Southern Baptist Convention is growing both in

the number of churches and in church membership, the Convention is not growing as rapidly today as it did a few years ago. The
Home Mission Board of the Southern Baptist Convention made a
study of the Convention for the period 1972-1977. During that
period of time, 59.1 percent of the churches grew in church membership, 39.4 percent of the churches decreased in membership,
and 1.5 percent of the churches experienced no change at all.
Although we are growing, we must be concerned for four out of
every ten are not growing.

The following highlights from the study of "The Unchurched
American" by the Princeton Religious Research Center are significant and reflect a decline in church attendance:

1. The report revealed that a high proportion of Americans
adhere to traditional religious doctrine and practice, but church
membership and churchgoing have declined.

2. An increasing number of Americans express their religious
concern apart from participating in the church.

3. Although most unchurched Americans had some religious
training, the same as the churched, the difference is that the
unchurched did not have religious instruction at home.

4. The key criticism of the unchurched is that churches have lost
"the real spiritual part of religion."

5. The study revealed that 52 percent of the unchurched say they
would be open to an invitation from the church community.

The last point opens the door to us if we are willing to go to the
unchurched in the Spirit of Christ.

According to the February 23, 1978, issue of *The Christian
Science Monitor,* church membership in England is down. Chris-
topher Andrae writes:

In 1975-76, the church commissioners authorized demolition of one
church every nine days. The Advisory Board of Redundant Churches
prophesied in its annual report for 1976 that between 1960 and 1980,
the total number of Church of England churches declared redundant
will be more than 1,000 and that this rate will either remain stable or
increase. In England and Wales, more than 650 non-Anglican
churches are recorded as having been closed in 1974-75. In the past

forty years, some 5,000 Methodist chapels have been shut. United Reform Churches, Quaker Meeting Houses, Baptist Tabernacles, Unitarian Chapels, Congregational Churches—all number losses.

In the face of slowing church growth, Southern Baptists have set themselves to increasing the number of churches from 35,000 to 50,000 by the year 2000 and are planning to share the gospel with every person in the world. This is Bold Mission Thrust.

There are critical spiritual needs in our world which must be met by God's people.

A Personal Burden

God will grow a world in our hearts if we will let him. Reading the four Gospels of the New Testament causes one to become aware of the burden Jesus had for the people of the world. He accepted no barriers and expressed his compassion for everyone.

Matthew reported that Jesus went about all the cities and villages to teach in their synagogues, to preach the gospel of the kingdom, and to heal those who were ill (Matt. 9:35). The compassion and concern of the Lord is pictured in the following verses:

But when he saw the multitudes, he was moved with compassion on them, because they fainted, and were scattered abroad, as sheep having no shepherd. Then saith he unto his disciples, The harvest truly is plenteous, but the labourers are few; Pray ye therefore the Lord of the harvest, that he will send forth labourers into his harvest (Matt. 9:36-38).

It is appropriate that I share my own personal testimony. God has been growing a world in my heart ever since I first came to know Jesus as my personal Savior. When God called me into the ministry, I surrendered with a view that I would go wherever he wanted me to go. As a pastor, God expanded the world in my heart. I felt there was a ministry that the church could express beyond its locale to the entire world. This process of enlarging my vision has intensified with each assignment God has given me.

However, I had not expected this process to be at work in a recent experience I had with a pastor from Seoul, Korea. When I served as the executive secretary-treasurer of the Florida Baptist

Convention, Florida Baptists accepted an invitation of the Foreign Mission Board of the Southern Baptist Convention, the Korea Baptist Mission, and the Korea Baptist Convention, to assist them in a major city evangelization thrust in South Korea. In planning for the three-year project, it was necessary for me to go to Korea. While in Seoul, I preached in the Yoido Baptist Church. The pastor of the church was a young, dynamic, and enthusiastic preacher. At the time, he did not speak English but through the interpreter he told me hè would be visiting the United States the following year. I invited him to visit Florida. He accepted. When he came to Jacksonville, we secured a Korean pastor to interpret for him. I invited him to speak to the Baptist Building staff in chapel the next day. He agreed. I said I would translate for him since the interpreter would not be available the next day! The interpreter wrote in English what Pastor Han, from Korea, planned to say.

The next day during chapel, the young pastor preached in Korean and I preached in English. A step at a time, we preached point after point of his sermon outline. It was an exciting experience. Then the pastor interrupted himself and said in broken English, "I speak now if okay with you."

Although surprised that he could speak English, I assured him that it would be perfectly acceptable. He turned to the chalkboard and drew a rough map outline of his part of the world. Then he came back to the pulpit stand and said, "I thank you for coming to Korea to help us reach our nation for Christ. Koreans like Americans, and we are grateful for your help."

Returning to the chalkboard, he explained the map he had drawn on the board. It was an outline map of China and depicted the close proximity of Korea to China. Then he said, "There are 900,000,000 Chinese who do not know Christ as Savior and the Chinese like Koreans. If you will help us reach Korea for Christ, perhaps, God will use us as Korean Christians to reach China for Christ."

This was the first time that I had even thought of the possibility of the Korean project being expanded to include China. With the enthusiasm of the young pastor and other Koreans, it might well be that God's plan to reach China includes Korean Christians going there as missionaries and preachers. With that experience, God grew another part of his world in my heart.

Faith to Get Feet Wet

Reflect again on the Scripture from Joshua 3. The miracle of the Lord would not happen until the feet of the priests bearing the ark of the covenant were in the river Jordan. When the priests stepped into the water, God worked a miracle and cut off the flow of the Jordan River from above. The priests stood firm on dry ground in the midst of the Jordan and the Israelites marched over on dry ground into the Promised Land.

We need to have faith strong enough to get our feet wet. Let me suggest some areas where our faith needs to be increased.

Praying. All of us are aware of the importance of prayer, but many times we fail to pray as we ought. We need to pray, and pray, and pray, until the fire falls. Remember the experience in the dedication of the Temple. When Solomon had completed his prayer, "The fire came down from heaven, and consumed the burnt offering and the sacrifices; and the glory of the Lord filled the house" (2 Chron. 7:1). Later God said to Solomon, "If my people, which are called by my name, shall humble themselves, and pray, and seek my face, and turn from their wicked ways; then will I hear from heaven, and will forgive their sin, and will heal their land" (2 Chron. 7:14). Praying will bind our hearts to one another and to God.

Preaching. Preachers of the gospel in the twentieth century are faced with difficulties never dreamed of in days gone by. Nevertheless, God's preachers are called on to pay the price in order to preach the Word. Great biblical preaching requires hard work and prayer. When preachers stand to preach the Word of God, they must have a message from the Lord. If a man preaches for thirty minutes to one hundred people and does not deliver a message from God, he has wasted at least fifty man-hours!

Working. The priests were enlisted to bear the ark of the covenant which was no easy assignment. It demanded personal involvement. As God's people, we are called on to work diligently through our churches in reaching this world for Christ. Church work is no place for a lazy person.

Loving. As God's people, and following the example of our Lord, we are to love until our hearts break. The Bible teaches: "They that sow in tears shall reap in joy. He that goeth forth and weepeth, bearing precious seed, shall doubtless come again with rejoicing, bringing his sheaves with him" (Ps. 126:5-6).

The church can be effective in this world, but the church will be successful only as it marches forward under God's orders. When we follow God and obey his orders, he will work miracles through us and all of the nations of the world will be blessed. We can and must become a blessing to the nations of the world.

What a challenge! What a victory! What glory!